Sleepwalkers
AND OTHER STORIES

Sleepwalkers
AND OTHER STORIES

The Arab
in Hebrew Fiction

edited by

Ehud Ben-Ezer

A THREE CONTINENTS BOOK
LYNNE RIENNER PUBLISHERS
BOULDER & LONDON

Published in the United States of America in 1999 by
Lynne Rienner Publishers, Inc.
1800 30th Street, Boulder, Colorado 80301

and in the United Kingdom by
Lynne Rienner Publishers, Inc.
3 Henrietta Street, Covent Garden, London WC2E 8LU

Library of Congress Cataloging-in-Publication Data
Sleepwalkers and other stories : the Arab in Hebrew fiction / edited
   and with an introduction by Ehud Ben-Ezer.
      ISBN 0-89410-852-2 (pbk. : alk. paper)
      1. Hebrew fiction, Modern—Translations into English.
2. Palestinian Arabs—Fiction—Translations into English. 3. Jewish-
Arab relations—Fiction—Translations into English. I. Ben-Ezer,
Ehud, 1936–
PJ5059.E8S54   1998
892.4'36080352039727—dc21   98-25852
                                                          CIP

British Cataloguing in Publication Data
A Cataloguing in Publication record for this book
is available from the British Library.

Printed and bound in the United States of America

⊗   The paper used in this publication meets the requirements
       of the American National Standard for Permanence of
       Paper for Printed Library Materials Z39.48-1984.

   5 4 3 2 1

Contents

༄

Contents

Acknowledgments

The editor wishes to thank Nilli Cohen, Moshe Dor, Geffrey Green, Donald E. Herdeck, Haya Hoffman, Rachel Lieberman, Yael Lotan, Lynne Rienner, Shin Shifra, and Alona Zamir for their help in the preparation of this book, in its various stages, for publication; and his son Benjamin Ben-Ezer, who typed most of the manuscript.

He also wishes to thank the Oxford Center for Hebrew and Jewish Studies in Yarnton, England, which provided him the time and atmosphere during his stay there as writer in residence to complete the book.

The assistance of the Institute for the Translation of Hebrew Literature in the publication of this volume is gratefully acknowledged.

"Under the Tree" by Shmuel Yosef Agnon is reprinted by permission of the Youth and Hechalutz Department of the Zionist Organization, English translation by I. M. Lask, first published in *Israel Argosy*, no. 6 (Jerusalem) in 1951.

"From Foe to Friend" by Shmuel Yosef Agnon is reprinted by permission of the *Jerusalem Post*, English translation by Joel Blocker, first published in the *Jerusalem Post* in 1958.

"The Prisoner" by S. Yizhar is reprinted by permission of Jacob L. Rycus, English translation by Violet Chulock Rycus, first published in *Israeli Stories* by Schocken Books (New York) in 1962.

"The Swimming Race" is from *A Rare Cure* by Benjamin Tammuz, English translation by Joseph Schachter, first published by Hakibbutz Hameuchad (Tel Aviv) in 1981.

"Facing the Forests" is from *Three Days and a Child* by A. B. Yehoshua, English translation by Miriam Arad, first published by Doubleday (Garden City) in 1970.

"Latifa" is from *Palestine Caravan* by Moshe Smilansky, English translation by I. M. Lask, first published by Methuen (London) in 1936.

Excerpt from the novel *Breakdown and Bereavement* by Yosef Haim Brenner is from the English translation by Hillel Halkin, first published by Cornell University Press (London) in 1971.

Excerpt from the novel *Refuge* by Sami Michael is from the English translation by Edward Grossman, first published by the Jewish Publication Society (Philadelphia) in 1988.

"Nomad and Viper" is from *Where the Jackals Howl and Other Stories* by Amos Oz. English translation by Nicholas de Lange, copyright © 1965 by Amos Oz and Massada Ltd., copyright © 1980, 1976 by Amos Oz and Am Oved Publishers, Inc. English translation copyright © 1981, 1976, 1973 by Amos Oz, reprinted by permission of Harcourt Brace & Company.

The English-language translations of *Breakdown and Bereavement* by Yosef Haim Brenner, *Rose Jam* by Esther Raab, "The Swimming Race" by Benjamin Tammuz, "Facing the Forests" by A. B. Yehoshua, *Refuge* by Sami Michael, "Sleepwalkers" by Jacob Buchan, "Cocked and Locked" by Etgar Keret, and *The Night of the Kid* by Shin Shifra are copyright © by the Institute for the Translation of Hebrew Literature.

Introduction

∽

EHUD BEN-EZER

The thirteen stories and excerpts gathered in this collection are best understood in the broader context of a hundred years of Hebrew literature portraying Arabs and the Arab world. Jewish writers, first in Europe and later in Israel, have presented dramatically differing interpretations of the Arab, ranging from romantic visions of the armed and courageous Bedouin astride his noble horse to an existential nightmare, a shadow cast from the innermost depths of the contemporary Israeli psyche. This brief introduction traces views of the Arab through different periods of Hebrew literature and tries to indicate how each of the pieces in this book fits into that broader picture.

In the Hebrew literature of the late nineteenth and early twentieth centuries, the Middle East exerted a romantic fascination, exemplified by images of the Arab and the Arab world. Early writers depicted Arabs as devoted farmers and courageous fighters. Ze'ev Yavetz introduced a new type of Hebrew youth in his short story "New Year for Trees" (1891). Shedding the traditional image of the pale and frail Jewish yeshiva boy, Nachman symbolized the transition from passivity and resignation in the Diaspora to *sabra* (native-born) assertiveness. This new Jewish youth emulated the Arab's love of the land and could also confront him in armed battle.

In addition to worries about the climate and new diseases, the Jews in turn-of-the-century Palestine had to contend with personal danger and insecurity. It was dangerous even to ride from one settlement to another. This danger was integral to the returning Jews' struggle to resettle their ancestral land. Thus, descriptions of Arabs ambushing Jewish travelers and the desperate struggles that ensued also filled the new Hebrew literature from the beginning. This was more than a reflection of national conflict: it was the

1

reality of life in a semisavage land, under corrupt Turkish rule, where the inhabitants—of whatever nation or religion—were never safe from sudden attack.

The Utopian Visions of Herzl and Binyamin

Theodore Herzl's *Altneuland* (1902), originally written in German, is indispensable for understanding the early Zionist approach to the Arab issue. Herzl visited Palestine only once, in 1898, and it was a brief, disappointing experience. The country, and Jerusalem in particular, appeared gloomy and depressing as he described them at the beginning of the novel, which opens in 1902. But he goes on to portray a utopian society set in 1923, by which time Palestine is flourishing, thanks to the economic and cultural riches that the Jewish immigrants brought with them. They create a model society, a cooperative in which all inhabitants enjoy full equality—Jews and Arabs, natives and new immigrants alike.

Herzl was convinced that Jewish capital and the economic growth it would generate would transform Arab society, so that an Arab national problem would never arise. The Arabs would willingly sell their lands to "the new society" and would be accepted as full-fledged members of the cooperative. They would be grateful to the Jews for improving their standard of living. One of the novel's Arab protagonists, Rashid Bey, is born to a wealthy family that has profited from the Jewish settlement. When asked, "What will happen to all the *fallahs* [farmers] who have no land to sell?" he replies:

> Whoever has nothing to lose, clearly has only gained. See all that they have gained: employment, good wages, a better life. There was no more pathetic and miserable sight than an Arab village in Palestine at the end of the nineteenth century. The farmers lived in shabby mud huts unfit for a pigsty. Babies went naked, un-cared for, and grew up like wild animals. Now all that is changed. The Jews drained the marshes, repaired the sewage and planted eucalyptus trees which restore the land, all with strong, local workmen, and paid them fair wages.

Rashid Bey takes his visitors on a tour of an Arab village, where the minaret of a small mosque rises on the horizon, and explains that "these people are now much happier. They make an honest liv-ing, their children are healthy and go to school. No one has harmed their religion or ancient customs. They have only benefited."

Herzl's utopia went no further than improving the miserable living conditions in the Arab villages and refraining from harming their religion and customs. The national issue did not exist for him. His vision was limited to the economic development that the Jewish immigrants would bring about.

We find a different sort of utopia in essays by R. Binyamin (the pseudonym of Yehoshua Radler-Feldman), who was a close friend of writer Yosef Haim Brenner and was later active in "Brit Shalom" and other peace organizations in Palestine.

In 1907, before Binyamin migrated to Palestine, he published his manifesto "Arab Prophecy" in Y. H. Brenner's London-based journal, *Hame'orer*. Written in high-flown biblical language, it predicted a pan-Semitic development in Arab-Jewish relations. Binyamin believed that Jews could, and indeed should, immigrate to Palestine, but without aggravating the national problem. His solution was based solely on intensive agriculture and orchards: increased productivity would provide a livelihood for more inhabitants. There would thus be ample room in Palestine for more Jewish immigrants, without dispossessing the Arabs.

Binyamin's vision of the future of the two peoples is epitomized in the following lyrical and emotionally charged passage:

> In the future he shall be as one of you, no different from
> yourself;
> You shall give him your sons and take his sons unto yourself;
> Your blood and his blood shall mingle and grow strong;
> Each to his own kind, one kind for all;
> We are brothers, several families of one people;
> I will soon see this come to pass.

His pan-Semitic approach in "Arab Prophecy" envisions the fusion of the two peoples into one Semitic nation, a theme that is echoed in later writers.

Dominant Themes in the First Two Waves of Immigration, 1878–1914

The shared Semitic ancestry is one of several motifs dominating turn-of-the-century Hebrew literature in Palestine. These motifs are of vital importance for understanding the formation of the new *sabra* hero as a literary type and his relations with the neighboring Arabs.

The encounter of the Jewish pioneers—the immigrants of the first two waves of immigration (known as the First *Aliyah* and Second *Aliyah*)—with the Middle East and with Palestine's Arab inhabitants gave rise to several motifs. The first is the shared Semitic origins of the two peoples and the etymological bond of the Semitic languages. This affinity came perhaps as no surprise to Jewish immigrants from North Africa, the Mediterranean, and Yemen, but it was a new idea for Jews who came from Eastern Europe. The latter discovered in Palestine that Hebrew and Arabic were cognate Semitic languages, and they imbued this discovery with a romantic aura.

Israel Belkind, a member of the *Bilu* Jewish pioneer movement in the 1880s, published a Russian-language pamphlet in this spirit during the First *Aliyah*. Entitled "Palestine in Our Time," it exerted a great influence on the Jewish immigrant-pioneers of the period. This significant and interesting motif reappears in Binyamin's "Arab Prophecy," mentioned above, and in other stories, including those of Brenner. It later grew into the "Canaanite" philosophy of the poet Yonatan Ratosh, who believed that the Hebrews had to liberate themselves from Judaism, and the Arabs from Islam, in order to create a single pluralistic secular state— an entity that would extend throughout the Fertile Crescent, dominated by the Hebrew language and culture, and become the United States of the Middle East.

The second motif is the fascination of Eastern European Jews with the picturesque deserts of the Middle East. This appears as early as Feuerberg's "Whither?" (1899), though the author never set foot in Palestine and the story was first published a few weeks after his death at the age of twenty-five. His rallying cry "Eastward! Eastward!" welled up from a desire to found a new and a pure world in the East, which would be the antithesis of the corrupt Western European civilization. The clean and virgin desert was the ideal setting for a new existence.

The third motif is the so-called Arabization of the inhabitants of Palestine. Some Jewish pioneers, among them several Hebrew writers, fantasized about revealing to the Arabs their original Hebrew roots. Jews had been living for generations in Peki'in in the Galilee and in Dir-al-Qamer in Lebanon. Was it possible, mused the romantics, that the Arab inhabitants of Palestine are our true brothers? Could they be descendants of the ancient Hebrews or the early Jews? We must bring them back to our common ethnic source and create with them a new Hebrew culture.

A fourth motif is the perceived similarity between the image of early-twentieth-century Arabs and the biblical Hebrew forefathers.

For example, when Nahum Gutman illustrated Bialik's biblical tales, he peopled them with the Arab stevedores and seamen of his Jaffa childhood. This is a widespread motif in the literature of the period, whose writers had studied Talmud as children, were well-versed in the Bible, and easily picked up traces of these sources in the local Arab and Bedouin agriculture and customs. Palestine had undergone fewer changes from the biblical period to the end of the first quarter of this century than it has done in later decades.

The fifth motif, that of the legendary tribe of Bedouin Jews of Khalibar (who might have been living in the Arabian desert even before the time of Muhammad), began with the waves of Jewish immigrants from Yemen, especially during the Second *Aliyah* period, in the early part of the twentieth century. Shmuel Yavnieli traveled to Yemen in 1911 and was active there in bringing Jewish immigrants to Palestine. They settled in the new colonies of Petah-Tikva, Rishon-Lezion, and Rehovot. The younger East European immigrants and writers of the Second *Aliyah*, fascinated by the return of the Yemenite Jews, began wondering whether there might not also exist a tribe of Jewish Bedouins who could be brought to the land of Israel.

Hebrew writers of this period saw the implementation of Zionism and of Jewish immigration as a transition from passivity in the Diaspora to action in the context of the Jewish settlement in Palestine. The image of the armed watchman guarding the Jewish settlement took on a romantic dimension and was a precursor of the nascent Israeli army and soldier. The Arab was nearly always the adversary, the enemy, in this struggle. At the same time, the concepts of courage, mastery of weapons, and power were also derived from the Arab, especially from the image of the armed Bedouin astride his noble mare. The antithesis of the feeble Diaspora Jew was the strong, forceful *sabra* youth, whose new image was created in a dialectical process of assimilating the Arab's qualities while simultaneouly scapegoating the Arab as an opponent.

Moshe Smilansky published his *Arabian Sons* stories (under the pseudonym Hawaja Moussa) beginning in 1906. His writings serve as the classic example of the romantic approach to Jewish-Arab relations. He did not turn a blind eye to the facts; on the contrary, he knew that the gulf between the two peoples would only widen and its consequences grow bloodier. The only alternative to this, he believed, was to find ways to bring about greater mutual understanding.

Smilansky's stories and much of his ideology expressed this view. He never forgot his own childhood encounter (just after

arriving in Palestine) with an Arab horseman in the dunes of Cae-
sarea in 1891: the Arab struck him across the face with a whip.
Still, though he was a farmer and a member of a Jewish defense
organization, he wrote appreciatively about Arab customs in a series of romantic stories, most of which do not deal at all with the
Jewish presence. He depicted the bitterness and strife within the
Arab and Bedouin society and the animosity between families or
tribes in love stories with themes like those of *Romeo and Juliet.*
These themes also appear in some of the well-known stories by the
native-born Sephardi writers Yehuda Burla and Yitzhak Shami,
who were familiar with the East.

Smilansky's "Latifa," published in 1906, tells of love between
a Jewish farmer and a beautiful Arab girl who works in his vineyard. Despite the romanticism of its beginning, this is a sad, even
tragic story. It implies that there is no real possibility for love between individuals of differing nations. Each of the heroes is irrev-
ocably trapped in his or her social, cultural, national, and religious environment.

The literature of the First *Aliyah* minimized the gravity of the
armed struggle, adhering instead to a policy of benign propaganda. Its readership lived mostly in the Hebrew-speaking centers
of Odessa, Warsaw, and Vilnius rather than among the few Hebrew
speakers living in Palestine. These writers feared that painting a
bleak picture of Palestine would deter potential immigrants, and
they preferred the ideal to reality. Thus, dangers were submerged
in stories that frequently described the Jew easily overpowering his
Arab enemy.

But we do find some danger signals in the writings of Yosef
Haim Brenner, who described the abyss separating the two peoples. Brenner viewed the romantic stories of Jewish-Arab relations
written at the time as self-deception, and as an indication of failure to cope with harsh reality and the roots of the conflict.

Brenner was unique among writers of the Second *Aliyah* since
he was aware of the bitterness and difficulties facing the Jewish existence in Palestine. He described Jewish life with ruthless self-crit-
icism. He also believed that assimilation was a danger in Palestine
as well as in the Diaspora, and that the East could swallow up the
Jews, rather than afford them a heroic new life.

In Brenner's view, Arabs were primarily the enemy, and their
treatment of Jews was simply a continuation of the age-old animosity toward Jews in the Diaspora. Brotherhood, the socialist
ideals of the Second *Aliyah*, seemed to him flimsy and artificial vis-
à-vis Jewish-Arab relations. In the grim, bitter reality of daily life in

Palestine, he found no signs of love or peace, neither between the two peoples nor between individuals from the two sides. As if to confirm his dark vision, he was murdered by Arabs during the riots of 1921.

The excerpt from Brenner's *Breakdown and Bereavement* included here describes the psychological state of the novel's hero, Yehezkel Hefetz, who goes mad when, with a soul overwhelmed by conflict dating from his years in the Diaspora, he encounters the problematic relations between Jews and Arabs in Palestine.

Between the Two World Wars, 1919–1939

Between the two world wars, during the Third *Aliyah* and later, the Jewish-Arab struggle revolved around the ability to cultivate and settle the land. The young Jewish hero was depicted as torn between the romantic appeal of the return to the ancient homeland and the bitter reality of trying to master it. Total acceptance of that reality involved more than adapting to difficult living conditions; it also meant experiencing three waves of bloody riots between 1920 and 1938.

Natan Bistritzki-Agmon's *Days and Nights* (1926) deals with Jews who yearn for a father-figure, and it casts the Arab in this role. The novel tells of a Jewish youth, a member of a new kibbutz group, who hungers for the company of his Arab neighbor, Sheikh Sa'id. The young man seems to be imploring Sa'id to assume the role of his new father in place of his real father, who stayed behind in the Diaspora. His hopes turn to bitter disappointment, however, when Sa'id rejects him and becomes his enemy instead. In the struggle between the romantic, biblical view of the East, and the bitter reality, a pessimism emerged that emphasized the grimmer aspects of the Jewish national experience in Palestine.

Violence and tension recur in such works as "The Hajj of Hephzibah" (1927) by Ya'akov Steinberg, "A Galilee Diary" (1932) by Shin Shalom, "Tanhum Scroll" (1942) by Yitzhak Sheinberg-Shenhar, and "The Wanderings of A'mashai Hashomer" (The Guard) (1929) by Ya'akov Rabinovitz.

However, "Juma the Simpleton" (1928) by Yitzhak Shami, "Under the Tree" (1941) and "From Foe to Friend" (1941) by S. Y. Agnon, and "Rose Jam" (1933) by Esther Raab also exemplify the literature of that time. The story by Shami, who was born in Hebron, is a marvelous example of a Hebrew writer's ability to identify with his Arab hero without relating at all to the national conflict between Arabs and Jews. Shami describes the life of an Arab village and the distress of its residents with extraordinary vividness and color.

Agnon, in his stories, seeks to show that Arabs might come to acknowledge the right of the Jewish people to the land of Israel, but that coexistence and even peace cannot be attained unless the Arabs despair of their repeated efforts to undermine Jewish existence in Israel.

Esther Raab, like Yitzhak Shami, describes suffering in Arab society. Though her story takes place in Cairo, where Raab lived during the twenties, the situation of the young betrothed woman, Clementine, is typical of the life of Arab women in Palestine at that time.

The Generation of 1948: War and Its Aftermath

A new generation of Hebrew authors emerged just before and during the 1948 War of Independence. In their stories, the Arab became a moral problem for the Israeli soldier, who is disappointed and frustrated that the Jewish national ideal failed to accord with the ideals of brotherhood and peace.

For the first time, Israeli-born authors are prominent in this literary generation, which was beset by an ideological crisis extending beyond the war itself and relations with the Arabs. The socialist pioneer youth movements in Palestine indoctrinated the younger generation with a mixture of Zionism and belief in the brotherhood of all peoples. They held a naive, Herzl-like belief that "the Arabs would come to accept our presence in Palestine, since we bring progress to the Middle East." They struggled to liberate Palestine from the British, whom they blamed for the trouble and killings. It was widely held that the British were trying to apply the principle of divide and rule in Palestine, as they had done with the Hindus and Muslims in India.

The War of Independence and the creation of the state of Israel in 1948 proved conclusively that the Arabs utterly rejected Jewish claims to a national homeland. It also came to light that, during the war and its aftermath, Israelis had committed such acts as killing prisoners and expelling Arab residents. In less than a year, that part of Palestine that became the state of Israel was emptied of most of its Arab inhabitants.

The moral crisis and social-demographic upheavals gave rise to works such as "The Prisoner" (1948), "Hirbet Hiz'ah" (1949), and "The Days of Ziklag" (1958) by S. Yizhar; "The Swimming

Race" (1951) by Benjamin Tammuz; and "The Treasure" (1949) by
Aharon Megged. All these works are marked by the ideological crisis of the war. Are we, too, guilty? Could we have acted otherwise?
The Arab in literature is now neither romantic nor alien and menacing. He has become a moral problem. The cruelty that the Israeli soldier committed in the course of his national struggle
causes him to question his own moral values.

The War of Independence left a deep-seated trauma in that
generation. Its youth, especially, had to face the killing and atroc-
ities committed by both sides and the disappearance of their
childhood world in Eretz-Israel (Palestine) before 1948. They were
unable to adjust to the new Israel, or to cope with the mass immigration and the changes in values.

Israeli *sabras* were alienated from the landscape itself and
from their human surroundings. Everything was utterly changed
as a result of the occupation or liberation of new lands in the 1948
war, the mass flight of the Arabs, the waves of Jewish immigration,
and the overnight building rush devoid of any trace of romanticism. It is significant that most of Yizhar's stories take place in the
1948 war or just before it: the world that had existed until that
time was destroyed before the eyes of his protagonists, and they
failed to adjust to the world that arose from its ashes.

The generation of 1948 was bewildered by the changing landscapes and values. Perhaps that was why they adopted what they
saw as Brenner's last will and testament, his pacifist story-essay
Mipinkas [From the Notebook], written only weeks before his
death, rather than the grim prophecies regarding the Arab issue
that emerged clearly from all his other writings.

The contrast between the pre-1948 world and the postwar reality was captured in Yizhar's well-known story "Hirbet-Hiz'ah,"
published in 1949:

> Sure, what did you think? Of course! I should've thought of that be-
> fore. Hirbet-Hiz'ah is ours! You say there are housing and absorption
> problems! Hooray for housing and absorption, and how! We'll open
> a general store, build a school, maybe a synagogue too. There'll be
> political parties, people will argue about all kinds of things. They'll
> plough the fields and sow and reap and do great deeds. Long live
> Jewish Hiz'ah! Who would imagine that it was once some Hirbet-
> Hiz'ah? We came, shot, conquered, burnt, blew up, shoved away,
> pushed and banished. What the hell are we doing here!

That generation remembered their childhood in the Jewish
community under the British mandate, living alongside the Arabs,

the orchards, the landscape of Eretz-Israel before 1948—all past
that was gone and done with. Now it was time for the sobering,
painful awakening from their Zionist-Socialist education and from
the belief in a synthesis between Jewish nationalism and brotherhood among the nations, a belief shot to pieces by the war:

> The cruelty of the world: Enough! But who am I asking? My own
> country gazes at me, my friends, my own people, they are all
> bearing down on me, staring at me: Kill nicely, dearest son, kill
> cleanly with a wide sweep of your arm, kill with all the good we
> gave you, all that we taught you, kill for us, so that we may finally
> have a nice, peaceful world—I will kill, oh, will I kill!

The young generation of 1948 paid a heavy price in the war.
Their education left them unprepared for the intensity of the
Arab resistance. They were unwilling—writers included—to admit
that they could not have persuaded the Arab inhabitants of Palestine and the neighboring Arab countries to accept the creation of
the Israeli national homeland. They experienced a strong moral
outburst of self-accusation that smacked of Israeli superiority.
They seemed to be saying, "Had we behaved differently, the conflict would not have come to this. It was entirely up to us, but we
misjudged the situation."

Yizhar's "The Prisoner," the most famous of the stories re-
flecting this type of moral dilemma, was first published in Novem-
ber 1949. The narrator's indecision, the result of an upbringing
that had inculcated him with a respect for human life, liberty, and
freedom of thought, is vividly described. Now he is shamefully incapable of action when faced with the possibility that an old Arab
shepherd, a prisoner, might be killed. The narrator's Hamlet-like
agony leads nowhere: his thoughts paralyze his ability to act. He
deliberates the question from one side, then the other; he invokes
his education and belief in humane compassion, then raises
wartime justification for ruthlessness. His deliberations never con-
verge with the prisoner's personal fate; there is no personal contact between them. The Arab exists solely as a moral dilemma for
the Israeli soldier: the choices are either to kill the prisoner or to
expel him and separate him from his family. The story is open-
ended: the prisoner's death is not described, though we may assume it does take place. In any case, the prisoner will apparently
never return to his herd, his lands and family, or resume the life
he led before the war.

Similar themes appear in "The Swimming Race," in which
Benjamin Tammuz argues that the killing of an Arab prisoner, to

whom the narrator lost a swimming contest when they were boys, is a moral failure; it stains the military victory and also is a harbinger of future tribulations.

The 1960s

For the next generation of writers, those who reached maturity after the establishment of the state of Israel, the Arab continued to figure as an inherent part of the Israeli's inner world, though no longer as a moral problem or as part of the war experience. The Arab is transformed into a menace to the Israeli's very existence, a shadow projected from the innermost depths of the Israeli psyche and preventing the Israeli protagonist from extricating himself from his predicament, from his imprisonment in a state of siege, from being surrounded by hatred.

The story "Facing the Forests" (1963) by A. B. Yehoshua stems from a deep-seated sense that the Israeli presence among the Arabs is an existential nightmare. An Israeli student writing a thesis about the Crusaders takes a job as a fire-watcher in the forests in the south of Israel. In the watchman's hut live an Arab and his young daughter. The Arab's tongue has been cut out. The forest covers the ruins of an Arab village whose inhabitants fled in 1948; the mute Arab once lived there.

A pervasive sense of oppression overcomes the Israeli watchman, a sense of impending catastrophe, as if a fire is about to break out. Strangely enough, he shares his apprehension with the Arab. One might say that the waiting drives both men crazy. The watchman throws a lighted match and cigarette butts into the forest, as though secretly hoping for a fire. The Arab hides oil cans in different spots in the forest; the guard knows this but does nothing to stop him. Finally, the Arab sets the forest on fire and it burns to the ground. As dawn breaks, the ruins of the former village are clearly delineated on the charred soil.

The demonization of the Arab figure ultimately expresses the destructive, dark side of the Israeli spirit. The watchman longs for the fire no less than the Arab, since the disaster affords a relief that is preferable to the tension of endless watching and waiting.

The watchman's reckless behavior attests to his loneliness and despair. Is he merely torturing himself, or is he a victim of his society's conditioning? This is a difficult question to answer. In "Facing the Forests" there are no moral deliberations, no ideological crises. The moral confusion typical of Yizhar's story of prisoners and banishment, and of the works of Aharon Megged, Benjamin Tammuz, and others of that earlier generation, is absent here. All has merged into an existential nightmare, devoid of illusions. This is perhaps the typical approach of the generation of writers whose lives were molded and determined after the war of 1948, in the first nineteen years of Israel's existence, surrounded by enemies.

In a story with a similar theme, "Nomad and Viper" (1963), Amos Oz describes Geula, a frustrated woman who lives in a kibbutz, and her encounter with a Bedouin shepherd. The Bedouin is a primitive, almost bestial creature, ugly and miserable. Nevertheless, he arouses her. It seems he might rape her, and she is attracted yet repelled by him—but nothing happens. At the end of the story, Geula is found lying on the grass in the evening, among the shrubs near her room in the kibbutz. She has been bitten by a viper. In this story, the Arab symbolizes the dark passions of the human soul. Geula's attraction and repulsion play out her instinctual rebellion against the dictates of Israeli society, Israeli daily life. The viper seems to fulfill what the Arab began. The dark side of the soul also harbors death and madness. The Arab apparently already exists there, where animal lust and irrationality dwell with death and the drive for self-destruction.

Amos Oz's "My Michael" (1968), written before the 1967 Six Day War, is the story of a woman student in Jerusalem. Hannah, who is married and has a child, is slowly going mad. The shadow within her and the growing madness revolve around her childhood playmates, the Arab twins Aziz and Khalil. Their presence grows strong in her hallucinations; they become terrorists, sowing destruction and death. Their empowerment grows in her imagination and reaches its climax at the story's end, indicating perhaps the protagonist's acceptance of her madness.

The twins are a metaphor for Hannah's suffering, rather than its cause. This should be emphasized so that the story is not misinterpreted: death, sexuality, madness, and the dark side of the psyche exist independently of the Arabs' presence. Even idyllic peace, the tumbling down of the barriers of hate, a solution to the Palestinian problem—none of these will free the Israeli of his or her human suffering and turmoil. These are the features of finite human existence.

But from the 1960s on, writers such as Amos Oz, A. B. Yehoshua, and others employed the image of the Arab as a fictional metaphor for the menacing shadow, the projection of Israeli fears and terror. The Arab was not portrayed as a real individual, or as a representative of an ideological or moral problem, but rather as an integral part of the Israeli waking nightmare. He or she has no separate, independent existence, no social, national, or mundane being. The Arab does not so much frighten as persist in disturbing, and does not allow the Israeli to live life beyond the cycle of national strife and war.

A sense of foreboding and constriction is typical of other pre-1967 works, such as "The Border" (1966) by Moshe Shamir, "The Battle" (1966) by Yariv Ben-Aharon, "Another Time, Another Place" (1966) by Amos Oz, and "Ants" (1968) by Yitzhak Orpaz. At the end of my own novel *Nor the Battle to the Strong* (1971) (which, like Orpaz's book, was written before June 1967), a young Israeli student commits suicide while serving in the reserves by throwing himself toward the hostile border.

The Arab issue and its stereotypical embodiment was internalized. The Arab's presence filters into the Israeli, though not necessarily as guilt or ideological crisis—rather, as a persistent, troubling menace. This angst replaces the earlier generation's moral deliberations.

The Arab in Hebrew Literature After 1967

Alongside the depiction of the Arab as Other, as the enemy across the border, Hebrew literature also referred to daily life in Israel. Jews and Arabs lived side by side in "Little Israel," which existed between 1948 and 1967.

These works frequently deal with the Arab national question as a class struggle fought by Arab individuals within Israeli society. The shared social milieu of Jews and Arabs is the context of Hemda Alon's "No Stranger Will Come" (1962) and Yehoshua Granot's "A Bitter Cup of Coffee" (1967). The national antagonism assumes, or wears, the aspect of social and erotic competitiveness, neutralizing both the menace and alienation as well as the moral dilemma. These works were not written with the romanticism of the past. They deal mostly with the struggle of Arab youths trying to enter Israeli society and their conflicts with national, social, cultural, and personal issues.

The June 1967 war, known also as the Six Day War, intensified this trend. Arabs became increasingly an integral part of Israeli life, no longer only images of strangers or nightmarish enemies. Their situation is reminiscent of that of Jewish intellectuals in the West or of Jewish intellectuals from Arab countries in Israel. Torn between different cultures and identities, they pay a price for every decision they make, which heightens their sensitivity and complexity. This is the case in the novels *A Locked Room* (1980) by Shimon Ballas, *Refuge* (1977) and *A Trumpet in the Wadi* (1987) by Sami Michael, and A. B. Yehoshua's *The Lover* (1977).

Fat'hi, the protagonist of *Refuge*, is a pampered poet of protest, adored by his Arab readers and Jewish girlfriends alike. He is at once pathetic and tragic; an Arab who has lost his identity in trying to enjoy the best of both worlds, he ends up being viewed with suspicion by all. His poetry supposedly reflects the spirit of his people, but in fact he is alienated from them. This is made grotesquely clear in his visit to Jenin. The Arabs of the West Bank consider Fat'hi an Israeli for all intents and purposes, almost half-Jewish, an anomaly. The Jewish women treat him the same way, a stranger, yet charming.

He lacks any practical aptitude, but his high self-esteem ensures that he will look after himself well. His national aspirations, should they ever come to pass, would destroy him along with the state of Israel. But he lacks the courage to leave the country and join the PLO like his friend Fakri. The Israeli setting in which he grew up is his lifeline—he is perhaps more at home there than in another Arab country or the West Bank—and he cannot give it up.

Fat'hi stands for the intellectual and nationalist Arab camp in Israel, whose every action and utterance is subject to the scrutiny of several different positions: that of the Jewish population of Israel, the Israeli left, the Arab population of Israel, the Arab left, the Palestinians on the West Bank, and the Palestinians abroad. In addition, there is the artistic yardstick whereby his work will be evaluated in the corpus of Arab literature, not only as the work of a famed poet of protest.

Fat'hi is a far cry from all the stereotypes of Arab individuals we have encountered until now, from those in Moshe Smilansky's stories, through "The Prisoner" by S. Yizhar, the mute Arab in "Facing the Forests," and many other Arab stereotypes that exist in Hebrew literature. Fat'hi is educated, sensitive, talented, a stranger who is "one of us."

The lives of Jews and Arabs in Israel have become so intermingled that in Jacob Buchan's "Sleepwalkers" (1989) the Arab is a Hebrew-speaking Bedouin who is an officer on the Israeli Border Patrol. At the heart of conflict is a woman; she symbolizes a homeland, a country, and a goal for the two quarreling nations, much like Luna in Tammuz's allegorical novel, *The Orchard* (1972).

The excerpt from *The Night of the Kid* by Shin Shifra dates from 1990, but the world of the Arab woman it portrays takes us back fifty years. Shifra identifies with the woman and with the Middle Eastern landscape and climate. Her story, while extemely local, is at the same time imbued with the tensions and ancient myths of the region from the biblical and prebiblical period. In this manner, the distinction between Arabs and Jews is blurred, and the universal human element of the woman's tragic fate is brought out.

Etgar Keret's "Cocked and Locked" is by the youngest contributor to this anthology. Keret, a rebellious and critical writer with a black sense of humor, is well liked by young readers. He is not suspected of supporting the Israeli establishment. Nevertheless, his story brings home the fact that the conflict between Jews and Arabs, between Israeli soldiers and Palestinian demonstrators, still exists in its full ferocity. Young people on both sides of the barrier continue to strike and be stricken.

The Arab as a living and breathing individual appeared in post-1967 Hebrew literature as the country became increasingly binational. Arabs are no longer the product of romanticism or of bitter reality, nor a moral dilemma for the omnipotent, guilt-ridden Israeli soldier. They are neither existential menaces nor a social-national problem within Israeli society. But there are two nations in one country—a homeland of contradictory yearnings, contradictory longing—locked in a bitter, constant struggle waged on various fronts. These stories offer no optimistic solution.

A More Optimistic Postscript

The analysis above, with its pessimistic conclusion about a hundred years of Hebrew prose in Eretz-Israel, was drafted before the first Rabin-Arafat meeting in September 1993, the Oslo agreements, the peace with Jordan, and finally the assassination of Rabin—a national shock that may, in the long run, strengthen the peace process between Israel and the Arabs. Now the question is: Have these landmarks launched us into a new Middle Eastern reality, one that will be reflected in literature?

If a new reality does emerge, it will perhaps be the fulfillment of Herzl's original prophecy regarding the relations between the two peoples, as described in *Altneuland* almost a hundred years ago. Herzl was convinced that economic prosperity and progress would prove stronger than nationalist animosity, of which he was scarcely aware. The oil-rich Arab countries were nothing but desert at that time, and Herzl's hope that an influx of Jewish capital would develop the land for the good of both Jews and Arabs may be compared to modern expectations that U.S. support for Egypt, Israel, Jordan, and the Palestinians will ensure a profitable peace for all.

We have seen the theme of unrequited love in Hebrew literature in regard to Arabs. It appears in the five motifs that animated the literature during the First *Aliyah*, described above. Natan Bistritzki-Agmon's novel *Days and Nights* expresses the disappointment of young immigrant pioneers of the Third *Aliyah*, when the Arab rejects them and refuses to serve as a father-figure. We have seen the romantic fantasies, and we have seen them shattered. Unfortunately, the historical perspective seems to justify the pessimistic outlook of Hebrew literature on this subject. Still . . .

In his speech before the Israeli Knesset in 1977, Egyptian President Sadat said that the psychological breakthrough in Israeli-Arab relations was the most significant of all. I believe the motif of "the ardent lover," the dream that the Middle East will embrace us with friendship and love, is again emerging among Israelis after years of disappointment with Arab rejection. Should the Palestinians accept us wholeheartedly and surmount the psychological barrier, all the practical details of a future solution would become easier.

The theme of unrequited love in Israeli-Arab relations resulted in one of our most deeply rooted collective denials: that of the problem of Palestinian refugees from 1948 onward. Even politically moderate Israelis had no hesitations on the subject, due mainly to the "all-or-nothing" position of most Palestinians. Today, however, the closer the Palestinians come to reconciliation, compromise, and coexistence, the greater becomes the willingness of Israeli society to consider solutions to the taboo issue of the refugees.

Should the Palestinians persist in reiterating their threatening, intransigent stand, and continue to wield terror—I fear the process of reconciliation will come to a halt, and no solution will be found.

Writers are conditioned by the past, its accumulation of pain and grief; writers are also conditioned by the old view of the Arab Other as hindering the Israeli "good life." Even writers allied with the peace camp express profound fear and horror, with negative descriptions of the Other.

But to encourage optimism, literature dealing with Jewish-Arab relations in the past must ignore what Brenner called the "bitter reality." One must be utopian, romantic, pacifist, willing to advance a cause, and to incur the danger of misrepresenting a reality too painful to represent. Literature that furthers a cause need not be chauvinistic or nationalistic, either in Arabic or Hebrew. It need not be patriotic literature that denies the rights of the "other people," becoming mere propaganda. Literature can promote a bias for peace, as well.

The peace between Israel and Egypt, between Israel and Jordan, and perhaps the imminent change in the relations between Israel, the PLO, and the Palestinian people, suggest that politicians on both sides are one step ahead of the writers, and less pessimistic.

The Arab-Israeli author Emil Habibi, recipient of the Israel Prize, once said, "The literary portrayal of Jews and Arabs, each in the works of the other, will not change even when we know one another better and write about each other as individuals—the change will occur only after a political solution is found, which will bring normalization and peace between the two nations."

I believe he was right.

Latifa

❧

MOSHE SMILANSKY

"**I**f you never saw Latifa's eyes—you don't know how beautiful eyes can be."

So I used to say when I was still a lad and Latifa a young Arab girl, hardly more than a child.

And I still say so, for all the many years that have passed.

It was January, the rainy season.

I was in the fields with a group of Arabs, preparing the ground for planting my first vineyard. My heart was in a festive mood, which seemed to be shared by all my surroundings. It was a fine bright day. The air was clear and calm, warm and invigorating. The sun stood in the cast, shedding a reddish early-morning radiance over all things; it was a pleasure to breathe, to fill the lungs to their utmost capacity. Everything around was green, and graceful and beautiful wild flowers nodded on the untilled hills.

Among the Arab women clearing stones and *injil* I saw a fresh face. It was that of a young girl of about fourteen, upright and agile, in a blue dress. One end of a white kerchief covered her head, while the other end fell to her shoulders.

"What is your name?" I asked her, wishing to note it down.

A small face, brunette and coy, turned to me, while two black eyes sparkled.

"Latifa."

Her eyes were lovely—large, black, flaming. The pupils sparkled with happiness and *joie de vivre*.

"The daughter of Sheik Surbaji," added Atala, a young Arab who was at that moment shifting a big stone. His remark was flung into the air as though casually.

"Like to two stars on a fine summer night . . . " Atala began lilting in his rich, strong voice, glancing mischievously at me as he sang.

19

Henceforth my work acquired a fresh interest for me. When I felt heavy or dejected I would look at Latifa, and my depression and melancholy would vanish as at a magic touch.

Often I would feel the gaze of Latifa as she watched me. Often I would feel the flashing of her eyes, and sometimes her gaze was sad.

Once I was riding to the field on my small gray ass. At the well I met Latifa, a pitcher of water on her head. She was bringing water for the laborers.

"How are you, Latifa?"

"My father will not permit me to go on working . . . "

The words came pouring from her lips, as though she were emptying her heart of something that had long been oppressing it. Her voice was sad, as though some misfortune had befallen her.

"Would you not rather stay at home than work?"

Latifa looked at me, her eyes becoming dim as though a shadow passed over them. For a few moments she remained silent.

"My father wants to give me to the Sheik of Agar's son."

"And you?"

"Sooner would I die . . . "

She was silent once again. Then she asked:

"Hawaja, is it true that your folk take but one?"

"But one, Latifa."

"And your folk do not beat their women?"

"Nay. How shall one beat the woman whom he loves and who loves him?"

"Among you the maidens take those they love?"

"Assuredly."

"While us they sell like beasts of burden . . . "

During those moments Latifa's eyes were even more beautiful, deeper and blacker.

"My father says," she added a moment later, "that he would give me to you, if you would become a Moslem . . . "

"To me?"

I burst out laughing in spite of myself. Latifa gazed at me, her eyes full of anguish.

"Latifa," I said, "become a Jewess, and I will take you."

"My father would slay me, and you too."

The next day Sheik Surbaji came to my vineyard.

He was an old man with a fine white beard, a tall tarbush on his head, riding on a spirited white mare that pranced and curveted beneath him.

He gave greeting to the laborers, who on their side all bowed to him with great humility and became silent. At me he threw an ill-tempered look, and he greeted me with a snarl in his voice. I responded with equal coolness. There was no love lost between the Colony and the Sheik, who bore a fanatic hatred toward the Jews.

When the Sheik saw his daughter his anger grew to fury.

"Did I not ordered you to cease going to the Jew?" he stormed.

And to the laborers he said:

"Shame upon you, Moslems, who sell your toil to the unbelievers!"

The stick in his hand fell several times on the head and shoulders of Latifa. Thoroughly angered, I made a motion toward him, but the sad, black, tear-filled eyes of Latifa looked at me as though entreating me to be still.

The Sheik and his daughter departed. The laborers breathed more freely.

"Sheik Surbaji is pitiless," said one.

"He is furious because he can no longer get his laborers at half the wages, and make them toil from morning to night. The Jews compete," said a second.

"And I know why he is in a rage today," said Atala, a cunning smile hovering about his lips.

Latifa did not return to work.

One afternoon a few weeks later, when I left the house where I was accustomed to take my meals, I met her. She sat on the ground outside offering chickens for sale. When she saw me she rose. Her eyes were more beautiful, and more sad than ever.

"How are you, Latifa?"

"Thank you, Hawaja."

Her voice shook.

And Latifa often brought chickens for sale, and always at noon hour . . .

One day Atala said to me:

"Hawaja, Latifa has gone to Agar; the Sheik's son has taken her—a small and ugly fellow . . . "

To me his words were like a stab in my heart.

Afterwards I heard that the house of Latifa's husband was destroyed by fire, that Latifa has fled to her father's house, and that they had taken her back to her husband against her will.

Some years passed. I was living in the house which I had built for myself. Other black eyes had made me forget the eyes of Latifa.

One morning I went out and found two Arab women holding chickens.

"What do you want?"

One of the women rose out from the ground and gazed at me.

"Hawaja Musa?"

"Latifa?"

Aye, this was Latifa; this old woman with her seamed and wrinkled face. She had grown old, but her eyes still retained traces of their former brightness.

"You have a beard—how changed—" she whispered, not moving her eyes from me.

"How are you? Why have you changed so?"

"All things come from Allah, Hawaja!"

She was silent. Then:

"Hawaja Musa has taken a wife?"

"Yes, Latifa."

"I would like to see her . . . "

I called my wife out.

Latifa looked at her for a long time.

There were tears in her eyes . . .

I have not seen Latifa since then.

(1906)

—*Translated by I. M. Lask.*

Excerpt from
Breakdown and Bereavement

YOSEF HAIM BRENNER

Part 1, Chapter I

It was an afternoon in the middle of April when the accident occurred. The year was a leap year, rainy and warm, and on that
summery spring day in the commune he had already been given
the job of getting in the hay. He and Menahem, the hired hand,
were at work in the field; Menahem up above, on top of the wagon,
and he, Hefetz, down below; Menahem at a leisurely pace, without
visible exertion, like all the migrant help who were one day in Dan
and the next in Beersheba,* and he, Hefetz, the regular member of
the commune, zealously straining every muscle, as had always been
his way, particularly since his last return from abroad. Rivulets of
sweat streamed down his face and his eyes shone triumphantly with
the effort, as if to say, "See, I too can hold my own!" He worked
without letup, tiring his partner and driving himself ever closer to
exhaustion with each bale of hay he pitched upward. Before Menahem, quick as he was, had finished setting one load in place, an
even bigger one would come flying at him like a mad bull.

The wagon filled bale by bale; the distance between the two
men grew gradually greater and with it, Hefetz's exertions. His
Arab *kaffiyeh*† slipped unnoticed from his head. The sun beat
down with its usual fierceness. Suddenly the man below uttered a
soft groan and staggered slightly with the load on his pitchfork.
Menahem looked down to see a large bale of hay, the heaviest yet,
overturned on the ground, and Hefetz squirming beside it. "The

---

*Dan and Beersheba were the northernmost and southernmost outposts
of Palestine at that time.
†The cloth head-covering commonly worn by the Arabs of Palestine.

23

devil!" he cried, slipping down from above. What could be the
matter? Sunstroke? Malaria? Chills?—No, a sharp pain . . . a pain
below the waist . . . ach, what an ass!

That evening the members of the commune assembled in the
kitchen and decided to send Hefetz to Jerusalem at the expense of
the sick fund. True, it was nearer to Jaffa, but in Jerusalem, it had
meanwhile been discovered, the injured man had some distant relatives. The elected head of the commune even recalled how several
years previously there had been some other trouble with Hefetz, on
account of which (Hefetz himself had not been consulted) it was
decided to send him to Jerusalem too, only then (how times had
changed!) there was no choice but Jerusalem, either Jerusalem or
Beirut, because . . . because in Jaffa they didn't have the right sort
of place for him . . . only meanwhile Hefetz had decided to leave
the country, which put an end to the affair. It seemed, though, that
a man couldn't escape his proper destiny. No, indeed . . .

Indeed, so it seemed. In the course of the evening two or
three other old workers also recalled Hefetz's journey abroad and
the events that led up to it. These were described most vividly by
"the Master-of-intrigue," a scarecrow of a man with two left thumbs
whose favorite tactic was to boast and threaten at once that he was
imminently about to receive a ticket for passage from his brother
in Brazil; in the meantime—for this had been going for five
years—he did his best to turn one friend against the other, and
particularly, to complain about the cook, who wasn't fulfilling her
duty, the duty of a cook in an agricultural commune in the Land
of Israel. Ah yes, Hefetz's madness. "I tell you, we should all have
the luck to be as mad as he was!" (If only his brother in Brazil
would come to his rescue already . . .) The business with Hefetz
had happened several years before. The commune was not then in
existence; in fact, there were no communes at all; in other words,
the new form of life developed by the pioneers in Palestine, the
agricultural collective, had not yet appeared on the scene. In those
days they all worked in the "colony," or more precisely, passed the time
there, Hefetz as well. Several days before the first night of Passover
("Hasn't anyone noticed? This time it's almost Passover too!") he had
fallen ill.* "Still, his illness then, gentlemen, was of a different sort."

---

*The first night of Passover is annually a time of tension for East Euro-
pean Jews. For Hefetz—as emerges later in the chapter—Passover is asso-
ciated with the traditional fear of pogroms and of the blood libel of Christian accusation against Jews of slaughtering Christian children and using
their blood in the baking of unleavened bread eaten on the holiday.

It was a nervous, a . . . what was the word? . . . a *psychic* disturbance. In fact, he seemed to have gone slightly mad. On the other hand, there was no need to exaggerate: he was far from completely deranged. In any case, there was nothing dangerous about his condition. What was it someone had said? Yes, someone had hit the nail on the head: it was the sort of illness that concerned the patient alone. It was an attack of . . . what was the word? . . . of *anxiety*.

"But it wasn't just that," added some of the other old-timers. Anxiety . . . of course . . . but in general . . . morale at the time was terribly low. It was a critical period, a time of transition, for the Jewish workers in the settlements . . . and Hefetz, who had a bad case of malaria, had been on a diet of quinine and was very weak. To be sure, there was nothing out of the ordinary about this; but because of his weakness and his inability to work during the day, he had decided to become a night watchman. The dangers of being a watchman, of course, were not then what they were now, but since his nerves were on edge and the work was new to him ("After all, he was no great hero to begin with," observed a voice from the side to the general approval of all) . . . on account of all this, it was said, he panicked one night while on duty and imagined he was being attacked. It was this fright that undoubtedly brought on his illness.

"In any case, you can't but feel sorry for him," remarked the Master-of-intrigue in an unusually mild tone. "It wasn't wise of him to go abroad. Others could have left at the time and didn't—and he could have stayed and he left. It all goes to prove that he was already out of his mind. After all, we all know that you have to be mad to want to leave this country, don't we, my friends? Still, looking back . . . abroad, you know, the cooks are better than ours, ha ha . . . say what you will, he came back with his belly full. He must have feasted like a king over there. What a character, that Hefetz! The man runs away, so it seems, because he's gone quite berserk, shows up again, I won't say recovered, but anyway, with some . . . what's the word? . . . *flesh* on his bones, and then goes and loses that too. And all in a few months. Our commune simply has no luck, my friends."

"But who's going to take him to Jerusalem?" asked the head of the commune deliberately interrupting the talk; his heavy eyes stared down at the ground, as they always did when it was a question of general concern.

The posing of a practical question led to discussion, dissent, innuendo. Those who were disinclined to make the trip to

Jerusalem with the injured man were quick to put forth their candidacy, offering to sacrifice themselves for the common good, while taking care at the same time to present their case in such a way as to make their going clearly out of the question; while those who would have been only too happy to take a few days off from work and see Jerusalem at no cost to themselves did their best to seem reluctant—though if duty called, of course, they would have no choice but to comply . . .

"Gentlemen, it's one o'clock in the morning," tired voices called out. "We've got to put an end to this." They had just resolved to cast lots when Menahem, the hired hand, volunteered his services.

This young man of twenty-two had already been "everywhere"; indeed, he had even met Hefetz once before some where in Western Europe, before coming to Palestine, and had taken a liking to him. Menahem's knowledge of geography—he could all but tell you the exact distance in kilometers between any two cities in Austria, England, Germany, France, even Belgium and Holland—did not come from books. He had a weakness for stations and train tickets and his favorite saying was: "The devil take it! Fish look for deep waters, men for sweet!" His eyes, though round as an owl's, were not owlish at all; they were merry, open, honey-colored, but not too sweet or cloying; they were rather like the honey that is fresh from the hive and still dripping bright with pure brilliance. Menahem took to new surroundings as no one else, plunging straight into them as into a clear mountain pond, lazily greeting each stranger with a fond hello, as though inviting him to partake of his honeyed essence. He liked to go barefoot and even took pride in the fact; yet somehow this failed to annoy Hefetz the way the exhibitionalistically barefoot types generally did. The simple, childish way he enjoyed things made up for everything. He liked to swear—"the devil take it!"—to stake all on an oath—"upon my life!"—to break into laughter, to gossip about the girls in the nearby village, to tell an occasional indecent joke (at times such as these Hefetz would become strangely pliant and laugh submissively); none of this, however offended a soul, for it was done without the slightest malice, in a comical, almost piping voice. "I don't like to talk about by troubles," he would say to Hefetz. "If talking about them could drive them away, why not? Then I'd talk about them all day long, I'd do nothing else, just like you. But as it is—I leave it to you . . . "

The debate over Menahem's proposal gathered strength. Those who were averse to going and feared to draw the unwelcome lot threw caution to the winds and declared (it was really too late to keep up pretenses) that it was only right for the hired hand, who had come with Hefetz from abroad, to go with him too; the opposing party, however, had persuasive arguments of its own, the most powerful among them being that a nonmember of the commune should be made to travel at his own expense. Menahem's acceptance of this last condition hastened the final decision in his favor.

And so Menahem went with Hefetz to Jerusalem.

On the way, as they approached Jerusalem, Hefetz thought he felt better and began to regret having come. The whole thing now seemed to have been something he'd imagined. Why must he blow up everything out of proportion? He had collapsed while at work—was that any reason to go running to the doctor? What an amateur he was at suffering! It was really just like him.

Menahem spit through his teeth in his fashion and tried to console him. If the condition wasn't serious, so much the better. The pain was real enough. Since he would be unable to work for a few days anyhow, what did he stand to lose?

Hefetz listened and felt reassured; still, he announced in advance that he had no intention of seeing a doctor in Jerusalem. The latter would only laugh at him, that much was certain, and he was not going to make a fool of himself. In fact, it had already once happened to him that he had thought he was ill and had actually been in great pain; by the time he'd arrived at the doctor's, however, the pain had disappeared and he hadn't known what to say! He wouldn't say anything to his relatives, either, simply that he had come to Jerusalem for the holiday. If he should have to stay a while longer, he could always tell them the "truth"; he was malarial, the quinine no longer helped; he needed a change of air, and so he had decided to stay in Jerusalem and not go back to the farm . . .

And yet, when all was said and done, he needn't have come. It was really just like him. Always on the run . . .

His trip abroad, for example—what made him take it? He had been about twenty years old when he first came to Palestine, strong, healthy, undemanding, a little bit odd perhaps, but still— popular enough. Elsewhere, abroad (in Hamilin's circle of students, for example), he had been a dull-witted, clumsy, solemn young man, at a loss to get on with the weaker sex and in general having no luck with it, in short: the very opposite of well-liked. No, elsewhere someone like him had no chance at all. In the workers' inn in the colony, on the other hand, surrounded by bearded, bookish, ascetic votaries of labor; there where everyone was an eccentric of sorts, a bit of an "original"; there and only there could he too, Hefetz, be a good companion, even if he wasn't contentious like the rest of them and didn't argue at the drop of a hat or take sides in every quarrel of play politics out of sheer boredom and the need to pick a fight . . .

And yet he went abroad. It was just like him. Even before that, all the time he was in the colony—a period of several years, all together—he had gone about with a strange feeling. He had felt as though he were trapped in a long corridor, but only for the moment; somewhere ahead was a room that was still to come, that had to come. He was incapable of saying or describing what this room was like; yet there was no end of fantasies about it, bizarre, impalpable, but sweet nonetheless. At any rate, it was clearly intolerable for things to go on forever without these dreams coming true . . . and not only because life as it was wasn't good and deserved to be better. Of course, he wanted this too, and at times the desire would actually get the best of him, but deep down it was not the main thing. The main, the overriding thing was . . . if only everything weren't so dry and bitter and hard: the burning, sweat-sucking air, the filthy inn, the sickening, poisonous food, the alien cold surroundings; it was impossible not to dream of a comfortable place to live, a good meal, shade, a cool stream, tangled woods, tree-lined streets . . . but in any case, it wasn't this that mattered most . . . on the contrary: sometimes he should deliberately resist the slightest improvement in his life, refuse to escape the desolation, the apathy, the packed quarters, the filth, even for a moment. No, what never failed to crush him was the utter pointlessness of it all: it seemed monstrous to him to have to go on living like this, for no reason, as a Jewish "farm hand" always looking for work; monstrous when he found it to have to go out every morning and compete with a horde of strange Arabs; monstrous to have to fight all day long with the ill-mannered foreman; and then to return to the inn at evening and gulp down a sour, gassy gruel that boded ill for the stomach; and afterward to drop by the workers' club to yawn once or twice and read an old newspaper; and then back to the inn again, to a bachelor's sleep bitten into by all kinds of bugs; and once more to rise with the ringing of the clock and work all day long until evening. And the work had no meaning, and the end was far, unclear, invisible, nonexistent . . . to go a year like that, two years, ten years, forever . . . and never any change; no relief, no progress, no hope . . . *What? Everyone lived that way,* Menahem said? Yes, of course, everyone did; his spleen and his ennui had been banal, of course, but he had suffered from them all the same. A kind of apathy had come over him, a total indifference to what he ate, the way he dressed, where he slept. He could have gone for months without changing his clothes or lain in an unmade bed from one week to the next and let his mind wander or not wander as it pleased. He loathed it when his roommates took the trouble to tidy up. It was a strange thing, his illness . . . the word "melancholia" did not exactly fit it . . . it was as though some horror of life had taken hold of him, a revulsion toward everything around him. Food disgusted him; he grew thinner every day, and the less he ate, the more he dreamed and talked, as if to escape his inner fears. He had never been much of a talker before.

What did he talk about? About everything except his unspeakable fantasies . . . *The darling little girl whom he has seen in the school in the colony would grow up to be a young beauty. A woman's grace, a man's strength, would join in her soul. One day she would be seventeen . . . and he would be thirty-five, twice her age, a weary castaway . . . but she would say: "It doesn't matter . . . I've seen all your suffering and I want to share it with you . . . Father is the richest man in the colony, and I'm the most beautiful woman, I know . . . But I'm leaving it all for you because it's you that I want . . . " No, she would not say it that way; she would not speak so commonly . . . She would put her hand in his without a word—everything would be understood, transformed into infinite bliss . . .*

Hefetz talked about practically everything during those terrible, garrulous days, but he did not talk about things like these, not about his wild, insane imaginings. As though by itself, with no effort on his part, his conversation turned to matters of the general interest—matters, that is, which might have pained him, even moved him deeply in ordinary times, but which at bottom, and especially now, meant nothing to him at all. The more remote a problem was, the less he or anyone else could do anything about it, the greater his concern. He talked a great deal, for example, about the Arabs; he spoke of their national awakening and of their hatred for the Jew; he was obsessed . . . by the possibility of a pogrom, over which he wracked his brain, soliciting advice and making endless plans for rescue and relief. Once an Arab woman from one of the families in the village had stopped by the inn, which was near her house, to inquire of those seated on the bench outside whether they had seen her little brother, who had gone off somewhere unannounced. He, Hefetz, who had been sitting in the doorway, turned as white as a shroud. He didn't attack her or lay

a hand on her—it hadn't yet come to that—but when he heard
the word *zrir,* meaning child, he jumped to his feet like a shot and
leaped backward over the threshold as though looking for a place
to hide, from where he began to stamp his feet and to shout: "*Zrir,
zrir,** I know what she's after! We're not cannibals here! We don't
drink human blood! But just try to convince her that we don't
have her brother when the Arabs are awaking and the germs of
hatred have infected them too . . . See where it gets you!"

Under the circumstances, as long as Hefetz carried on this way
his companions were understandably not upset; they saw that he
had changed, of course, but while his preoccupation with the
common good lasted, they did not give it much thought. They
were all, after all, neurasthenics, cosmic worriers, who bore the
world's burdens on their shoulders and judged everything in
terms of the group. If one of them traveled abroad, for example,
he had not simply gone someplace else, but had "given up" and
"betrayed the ideal"; if someone stood guard in a vineyard he was
not just a lookout, but "a watchman in the fatherland"; if the cook
burned the food in the inn—and when did she not burn it? and
who really cared, anyway, except that it was something to talk
about?—she was an execrable cook, of course, but she was also "an
irresponsible woman with no sense of duty to her comrades."

Soon, however, a reaction set in and everyone realized that
Hefetz was not just another victim of general conditions. His final
metamorphosis made this apparent. He looked as unwell and distracted as before; but now not only his mind, but his tongue too,
seemed to have gone out of order. It was all very well for him not
to talk, but there was silence and there was silence! For days on
end he refused to say a word. It then became obvious that his pre-
vious chatter had been one thing, his illness another, and that the
latter derived not from the common predicament, but had private
origins, underlying irritations, which were purely personal in nature and had nothing to do with anyone else. Only what was to be
done? During several meetings held in the sick man's absence,
though not without his knowledge, much was said about the need
for treatment, namely, for "bandaging up the old wounds" that had
come open and begun to bleed again, etc., though at the same
time, of course, a "permanent cure" was perhaps "out of the question," "but as a temporary measure" . . . Jerusalem or Beirut . . .

But when Hefetz, overcome by inner desire, sheepishly announced that he was about "to take a trip," in other words, to go

*Arabic: little child

abroad completely, respect for him reached a new low. As always, it was a time when the number of workers who came and went far exceeded the number of those who stayed; still, the custom persisted, and not always as a mere matter of form, to grumble aloud about all those who "fled the field of battle" and betrayed the national cause . . .

Hefetz was ill . . . but with what? Hefetz was going . . . but where? To others he murmured that he wished to see the world a bit, but to himself he would add: *I want to live, to live.* In spite of the privileges conferred on him by his illness, he didn't, he couldn't, tell this to anyone else; he himself, however, was perfectly aware of the drives that impelled him—primitive, ugly drives, if you will, which in any case would never, could never, be fulfilled. Yes, he was tired of this monotonous, unbearable life, without a spark of pleasure, without a woman; he had to free himself of it, somehow cast its yoke from off his neck. Even his distant, feckless dreams had come to disgust him. He knew them only too well . . . *There in Europe there were great cities with all the good things of life . . . There was no end of possibilities . . . He would get a job, he would work hard, harder even than here . . . But the pay would not be bad . . . And at night, after work, his time would be his own, to do with as he pleased . . . He would enjoy himself, he would live like a human being and forget all this . . . He would walk the streets in the evenings, visit the music balls, the theaters, whatever he desired . . . There would be piquant, fantastic encounters . . . And other houses, too, which he would not shy away from . . . Perhaps he might even meet a gentle, attractive young girl . . .*

Part Two, Chapter II

The black-skinned wife of the Arab watchman focused on him with the whites of her eyes, then opened the small gate in the fence for him with her huge key. The mass of cliff-like boulders in the field across the way met his glance: to the north, in the crimson glint of the rocks piled before him, their color heightened by the reddish beams striking against them from low in the southwestern sky—it was nearly four o'clock and the December day was already on the wane—there was no suggestion of a father's forgiveness or a mother's sheltering breast, but neither was there anything sinister or somber anymore. Just a few days before he had paced wildly about in the garret above him, and softly groaned "rocks, rocks, rocks" without knowing why . . . knowing only when he did know that he would not be killed by the mob . . . it was enough that he had been imprisoned on a false charge . . . a charge brought against him by the Arab woman in the colony . . . before the Passover . . . the woman who had lost her child . . . And he knew then too, knew he would prove that his blood wasn't Jewish at all . . . Gentile blood flowed through his veins . . . he had been born exactly nine months after the first pogroms . . . he wasn't a Jew at all, but a *goy*, eighty percent Slav . . . how could the woman not understand that he didn't have her *zrir?*

He had been obsessed by strange fantasies like these, terrified by his own weird dreams. What had he imagined these rocks to be when he had stared down on them from above, his shirt hanging open, his nerves shattered, his mind in a fog, gripped with fear? At the moment he neither remembered nor wished to remember. All that was over with. The dread concealed in those groans . . . yes, he could feel it even now . . . only now it was over. The gate was wide open. He stood with his suitcase, his old companion, in one hand, wearing his own worn street clothes in place of the long, torn hospital frock which he himself had ripped, completely on his own, leaving it all, inmates, institution, everything, behind him. In another minute he would turn to the right and walk east, toward Sha'arei Yehudah, Mishkenot Yisrael, Oholei Ya'akov, hardly recognizable to anyone who hadn't seen him during the six long months of his imprisonment. *Onward to freedom then! Fresh air at last . . . and the rocks?* He watched their outlines blend with the backs of the goats browsing down the hillside among them. The sunlight turned everything the same golden red . . . No, it was pointless to groan. The rocks were just rocks. Soon they would recede into the distance and be gone.

Behind him the watchman's wife shook her head. "Look how the poor devil runs! How happy he is to be gone."

"And little wonder!" It was the head attendant who spoke in Hefetz's defense, a Syrian Jew whose pockmarked face and burly waist, so un-Jewish in its powerful girth, made him seem someone special, one of a kind.

Unconsciously, Hefetz slowed his steps to listen to the voices behind him. "Go, go and God bless you!" The Syrian urged him on deliberately but gently. "And don't look back! Be healthy and whole. Just don't talk too much, don't talk any more than you need to . . . and don't look where you needn't either . . . take my word for it . . . keep a tight grip on yourself. I've got nothing

*Arabic: little child.

against you . . . you can consider me your friend . . . take care not
to say any more than you have to."

And again the attendant made a point of stressing his friendship, as though there were reason to assume that Hefetz could not
help but doubt it. But the latter, though his well-wisher's words
meant little to him, bore him no grudge for what had happened
in the hospital. Indeed he could not have, for at the moment of
his release all that had slipped his mind; it was only an instant
later, when he was already through the gate, when suddenly *she* appeared out of nowhere from the side, as though to talk down the
attendant this time too, and to get at him, Hefetz—it was only
then that the memory flared within him . . . why, it had been like
that then too . . . when he'd been beaten . . . then too she had appeared like that out of nowhere, from the side . . .

" . . . *to beat a sick man like that . . . and such a quiet one . . . it's sheer
murder . . . "*

*"Such a quiet one, such a quiet one!" The attendant furiously mimic-
ked the nurse's aide from the women's ward, who refused to mind her own
business. "He tears his clothing to shreds . . . he fouls his food . . . "*

*"But I told you that he didn't eat tomato stew. Why did you have to
give it to him?"*

*"I gave it to him because I felt like it. And if he doesn't want to eat—
fine, he doesn't have to—but no games with the food!"*

*"As long as a patient isn't harming anyone else, one has to show re-
straint. The idea is . . . "*

*While he, the subject of the discussion, the object of the blows, reasoned
out loud in an imploring tone of voice as though he really weren't in the
least bit mad at all:*

*"Tomato stew . . . to mate or stew . . . so that's it, is it? But I'm a bro-
ken man . . . bric-a-broke . . . above, below, between . . . the heart is between . . . the heart is at the heart . . . but to stew? To eat is a sacrament,
the greatest saints worry that there won't be enough . . . for everyone,
everyone . . . that is, for every one of them. Only you mustn't call it socialism! Never! To hell with socialism! Everything all planned and
arranged and decided in advance—pooh! What a lot of nonsense—they'll
never get it right! The planners will take the pudding for themselves—of
course they will! Only of course, there should be enough to eat too . . .
enough for myself and my neighbor . . . and you're giving me stew? Wasn't
I created in God's image too? Er and Onan* abused God's image—it's all*

---

*The sons of Judah, of whom it is related in Genesis 38 that the latter,
rather than fulfill his levirate obligations to his deceased brother's child-
less wife, deliberately cast his seed to the ground.

in the Bible, the Humishl isn't ashamed to say so—the bastards stewed in their own juice. Bastards, not bastards . . . all of us are bastards, none of us are bastards . . . there aren't any bastards, so those who aren't mustn't feel proud . . . it's just that it says: 'And the sons of Judah did evil in the eyes of the Lord.' And myself? Good, evil, it's not that I deny it, it's just that I don't understand, don't know . . . I don't deny that I'm ill . . . that I need to be in the hospital . . . 'And it came to pass on that day'—that the whole world was put in a hospital. But in prison? Is that any place for me? Here, where even the prisoners' horses eat halvah?"

"What? Their horses eat halvah?" The attendant winked at the meddlesome nurse's aide and grunted twice in triumph under his breath.

The patient hastened to explain. *"That is, I didn't mean to complain. Halvah without bread . . . halvah with toadstools . . . it has to be, of course . . . there are worse prisons in the world than this. In* The House of the Dead* it's far worse . . . they suffer more there. But the things you give me to eat—it's just too much for me . . . believe me, it's too much! There are so many prisoners—and only one of me . . . how can you give me so much? A glass of plain water would be enough . . . water without milk . . . and an onion if you happen to have one . . . an onion . . . it can't do any harm . . . but no tomato stew. I'm not what you think . . . the doctor can say what he wants . . . you mustn't listen to him . . . "*

"We mustn't?" she asked curiously. "We mustn't listen?" She bent over to fix his cap, pressing against him with her long, thin body, breathing on him with her mouth. "Do you mean the doctor is wrong?"

"What is it you're suggesting? That I'd rather stew? Tomatoes! Feh, what ugly names these Italian vegetables have . . . of course! It happened in Italy . . . it's quite a story . . . "

And he proceeded to tell her the whole long story, which concerned a poor Italian who was a total failure in life, a man who had nothing to give. They had done their best to help him; he had been in great misery; he had wandered about for years, he had tried to escape his fate—but he couldn't avoid it. The inevitable happened. Sooner or later the wheel must come round. Four years went by—and the same thing happened again. What good had being in Italy done him? . . . had she heard the song about the farmer's wife? La, la, la, la, the farm-er's wife, la, la, la, la, la, the farmer's wife . . .

"How does the story end?"

—The end was simple. He had nothing to give because he was poor; poor and weak and terribly unhappy. But his love for life was even greater than his poverty and it triumphed. Because the poor Italian loved life, and even more than he loved it he felt rooted in it, rooted just like an onion.

*Dostoevsky's novel of Russian prison life.

The whole trouble was that here, in Palestine, he hadn't seen a single
onion. Not one farm grew them . . .

"La, la, la, la, the farm-er's wife . . . "

And he was off again on another tack:

"They say that Palestine is the center of the world . . . what a joke!" Why,
he himself was the center! In his present incarnation he was . . . a central
switchboard. That is, every time they pulled the switch he tapped his head
and another telegram arrived. The telegrams came flying from all over and
each one announced that its sender had gone mad. Burning wires led to him
from the far ends of the earth to transfix him and tell him everything . . .

. . . Yes, word had been received: the widow in Italy had lost her husband and was left with her six children, not counting the girl. The girl
didn't count at all: she simply got in the way, she made a nuisance of herself, she sang "The Farmer's Wife." She was in a stew over Hamilin, she
did whatever she pleased—the tomatoes were for her! But the six children
were hungry, they lay sick, three in a bed. The oldest was ten, the next
nine, the third eight, the fourth six, the fifth four, the sixth three, and she,
the mother, made seven! Yes, he knew how to count, he was almost a socialist, he wasn't crazy at all. And they were all hungry, naked, sick . . .
Hamilin had studied medicine but there was nothing he could do . . . there
was no one to help. Even he, the poor Italian, couldn't help. Seven wires
transfixed him (the girl didn't count at all): the first was ten cubits long,
the second nine, the third eight—but the fourth, what was the fourth?

"The fourth? The fourth what?"

"What makes you think that just because I have no visitors the world
is dead? You're wrong! I know everyone and I visit everyone . . . at night
. . . in the dark pit at the bottom of my dreams . . . rock bottom . . . a pit
full of eyes . . . my friends' eyes, people I know . . . the eyes of the other prisoners . . . what, you don't believe me? You mustn't think . . . life hasn't
come to an end . . .

All of a sudden, as though he were in complete possession of his
senses, he went on:

"Nothing here says anything about the world. It doesn't prove a thing
about life itself. Here it's just the broken little revolver of little man. What
is man that Thou shoulds't remember him? An individual. A single sick
individual. And an individual has no right to judge the mass of men. An
individual can only say: 'What have I to do with them? If I'm unhappy—
well then, I must be hard to please'. But the others are right too. 'So you're
unhappy, are you? Of course, you can tear your hair out if you like, but
what are we, the mass of men, supposed to do about it?'"

And just as suddenly his face went foolishly blank again:

"It's just that the world hasn't gotten any clearer! Life hasn't come to
an end—but the world hasn't gotten any clearer! The central switchboard

is all confused. The telegrams make no sense . . . the telegrams from the front make no sense. It's dark here in the pit . . . there's not a ray of new light . . . only without the switchboard it would be even worse . . . a bare bit of truth gets through . . . a bare bit gets bared . . . the naked truth . . . you can give a man tomatoes but you can't make him stew. I'm not what you think . . . not even Onan . . . Kenan not Onan . . . because Kenan begat Mehalalel and Mehalalel begat Jered and Jered begat Enoch . . . and Enoch Ezekiel . . . dost mean Ezekiel the priest, son of Buzi? Why, nothing of the kind, nothing of the kind! Just plain Yehezkel. 'And he shall set the stumbling-block of his sin before him.' He said that too, Ezekiel . . . "

(1920)

—*Translated by Hillel Halkin.*

Rose Jam

∽

ESTHER RAAB

The wild pigeons are cooing in the massive pepper trees. The sun rises and gilds the flat roofs; the columnar stems of the palm trees cut up the sky. The house gardens release the last of their night scents before the day grows stronger. The still-moist jasmine climbs and opens myriad eyes upon the fences; mossy shade still lingers in the thickets of wild rose and mango trees.

The vast, transparent, desert sky hovers, soaring from moment to moment over the long, shallow, white streets whose far ends merge with the horizon. The black-winged laban sellers are already pouring their mournful warbling sopranos into the dewy morning. Coming up immediately behind them are the Nile fishermen bearing damp baskets on their heads, proclaiming their simultaneous arrival in all parts of the city with a sharp, startling cry . . .

On the track leading up from the Nile, a caravan of men, women, and donkeys crawls across the yellow sheet of the desert; the air is pure and clear and the caravan's every move is visible from afar; like a trail of ants, the miniaturized creatures cross the canvas, laden with the fruits of the oases: milk, dates, and vegetables from the fat banks of the Nile that spread like green plush carpets verging on the dry wilderness.

Sixteen-year-old Clementine lay on a heap of white pillows under a diaphanous net, looking like a sweet dark ladybug. Her black eyelashes dominated her face like two fringes of soft unravelled silk, and her brown, slightly fuzzy cheek was almost violet under the dark flush. She spread her slim arms languidly and stretched herself toward the light—for this was the "sweet day," the day of making jam, rose jam. Clementine loved this day, she had a special gown for the occasion that was all fragrance and

37

sweetness. The dress was rosy, and sweet was the body with the budding breasts bursting out of it. Her plait hung down like a black whip, and at its tip the rose bloomed again in the form of a heavy knotted ribbon.

Inside the ancient garden with its marble fountains there was an avenue of rose bushes, full of big fleshy roses like little cabbages. The "sweet day" brought in a throng of shiny dark houseservants with their wives and children. With fingers black as beaks they plucked the roses, heaping piles of them on the reed mats, while the fire blazed and smoked and boiling sugar bubbled in the copper vat.

The whole assembly was supervised by the straight-backed old mother, dressed all in black, her two braids, remnants of her youthful glory, spilling from her kerchief and bouncing on her back; her gaunt face was fiery, while with her voice and arms she commanded the "sweet day."

Mohammed, the youngest servant, an elongated Berber with arms and legs like slender iron bars and a narrow burnished skull the color of bronze, took off his outer garment and now and then, addressing his comrades in the Berber tongue that sounds like scattering coins, cast a beaten dog's glance at Clementine, who was flitting from rosebush to rosebush in her "sweet day" gown. As the heat grew overpowering, Mohammed removed his waistcoat also, remaining in his white undergown.

The sun rose higher, seeming to capture the air with unusual speed, and its flames licked the desert sand; the green patches, the villages dotted here and there, faded and disappeared in the incandescent sea of sand.

The jam in the vat spread a hot intoxicating fragrance, the odor of roses. "The scent of woman," the people here call it; the maidservants gathered in the shadow of the house, and the basketfuls of rose petals still awaiting preparation, looking like dead butterflies, gave off a stronger perfume. The infants who had played underfoot all morning began to cling to their parents as sleep weighted down their little black limbs.

Then occurred the strange and awful thing: Clementine gave the order to bring up the glass jars from the cellar to fill them with the new-made jam. She was standing in the dank dimness of the cellar when all at once Mohammed appeared beside her, as if sprung from the ground, grasped her bosom with one movement, squeezed her small breasts with iron fingers that wandered all over her body; like a mad black insect, his hand buzzed over her gown which looked white in the dusky cellar; they were both steeped in the odor of roses, and she stood as if petrified, unable to move a limb, so obvious yet dreadful was the occurrence that paralyzed her. At that moment someone blocked the light from the entrance and Mohammed recoiled; his small daughter rolled down the cellar stairs and burst into sobs: a kick and a muttered curse, and the little one was thrown out. Clementine rearranged her hair, smoothed her gown, and carried out jars, which rattled in her tremulous arms . . .

Clementine is betrothed to tall pallid Naguib. It is said that he smokes opium, and moreover has brought a mistress from Paris, but he is a European, almost a gentleman. Except for his loud ties and nimble gestures, there is no difference between him and Mister James, who lives in the compound.

She has only seen her intended on the evening of their betrothal, when he gave her the ring that now glitters on her finger. "Her betrothed is upon her"—she fears him, as her companions fear their husbands and bridegrooms. She knows about this thing, has known all about it since she was thirteen, and realizes that by night and even by day he will drag her to his bed, as happened to her elder sister. She remembers how her sister ran away a week after her wedding and returned to her father's house, her eyes staring out of blue circles, trembling all over under the burden of her pearl necklaces and gems. But she went back to her husband and now her house is full of children; she is pale and worn out like all her twenty-five-year-old companions, and her husband's second wife lives in the same house as she. Clementine knew all this—and here was this black slave, like an ancient Egyptian deity from the museum in Cairo.

There was no wind. The clusters of dates seemed fixed in the white-hot heavens, the wild pigeons hid in the thick foliage or came down to dip in the pond. Out in the wilderness of sand a few solitary figures moved like ants which had lost their way. The distant Nile had stripped off all its misty veils, and its water flowing through the palm groves grew heavy and blue. Sailboats like white feathers glided over it past the palm trunks and disappeared up-river on their way to Upper Egypt.

In the rooms the mosquitoes rested unmoving on the ceiling, waiting for the night. So complete was the silence, that when one of them spread its wings and dived, its long solitary hum sounded like a fanfare.

Clementine fell asleep in the corner of the divan, her embroidery drooping in her lap. Little beads of sweat sprang on her forehead. Her sister's children lay sprawled on the rugs, fast asleep, breathing the hot dry air through their open mouths. The whole city slept, only the distant cry of a vendor could be heard from the empty white streets, like the buzzing of an early mosquito. The shutters filtered out the white outdoor blaze, and only when their slits turned ruddy did the denizens in the houses know that evening had fallen.

Now the palms cast long stripes of shadow across courtyards and whitewashed houses, the date clusters shook slightly, and in one of the blank walls a window opened, a dark head appeared and sniffed the air—the Nile was liberating cool moisture into the dryness. One by one the windows opened. Voices were heard all around. Chairs were carried out to the broad verandas, as well as cups of fragrant coffee and smoking narghillas; the sellers of mangoes and roast almonds cried their wares, and were answered by humble echoes from the blank walls.

Clementine's delicate nostrils flared, she threaded a fresh jasmine into her black hair and began to romp with the little ones— they climbed on her and she teased them, till at last she caught the most adorable of them, "Ya'alabi, ya ruhi," ya habibi, and showered passionate kisses on the squirming, squealing infant in her arms . . .

(1933)

—*Translated by Y. L. H.*

Under the Tree

SHMUEL YOSEF AGNON

Once upon a time I was fetching saplings to Degania. On the way I got off the ass in order to rest. Looking round I saw a worthy pasha sitting himself under the olive tree. I greeted him and he greeted me in return.

Where are you going? said the pasha to me.

To plant a few trees on our land at Degania, said I to him.

The day, said he, is still long and the sun is hot, sit with me for a while and let us have a chat. I went and sat down beside him. The pasha looked at my sapling and asked: A fresh fruit?

With your permission, sir, said I to him.

The pasha nodded and said, you are training the country well, experiment after experiment, plant after plant, tree after tree, vegetable after vegetable. I shall be surprised if you come to lack anything at all in it.

We do what is possible, said I.

The pasha nodded and said, and the land repays you. It seems to me that the land obeys you alone.

Your kindness opens the heart, said I.

Thereupon the pasha began praising Israel who transforms the wildernesses of Eretz-Israel into gardens and groves, and multiplies villages and dwelling-places in the country. Now I nodded in agreement with him and said to myself: When Israel is on the land, even the other nations praise him. Happy is he who devotes himself to the land and engages in its settlement, for all who devote themselves to the land and engage in its settlement devote themselves and declare the unity of His Great Name in Heaven and Earth and increase the honor of Israel, like a plant that is put into the ground and flourishes and mounts aloft.

I see, the pasha now said to me, that you are wise and He who made you gave you knowledge. So I shall ask you—tell me, to

41

whom is this land appointed and who will take the ruling of it over in the future?

I considered to myself what answer I should give him. If I were to tell him "The Earth is the Lord's and the fullness thereof," meaning that the Lord had given it to whom He saw fit, then there is the other verse: "And He gave the Earth to humankind," which could be taken to mean that the Lord had given it to those men who dwell therein. And if I were to tell him that he who seizes power therein would continue to be in power—that would be a deceitful answer, since this land is ours and the Holy and Blest One is going to return it to us in the future, and no nation of tongue can rule therein save Israel. So I said to him: Do you need me, sir? Why, surely you know to whom it was that the Holy and Blessed One gave the Land of Israel, and to whom He has promised to return it.

The pasha lowered his head between his knees and answered nothing. I thought that I might have annoyed him and said, It is not I who said it, but the Torah which declares it.

The pasha raised his head and said: I am one of the few remaining generals of our Lord and King the Great Sultan, may he rest in peace and blessing. Many a city did I lay waste in his name, many people did I slay in his honor. I taxed whole provinces and earned myself a great name in the name of the pitiful and ever-merciful God, and Allah viewed me favorably and opened His hands and made me satisfied. But when I had come to think that the world was created only to rejoice therein, the sovereign powers attacked our Lord the Sultan and went to war against him. I remembered my victories, with the regiments of soldiers roaring and shouting and trampling. Thereupon my fate sped me to go out to war against the enemy, whether to win or be defeated. I left my home and kissed my children and went to our Lord the King and kneeled down before him and entrusted my soul into his hands, saying: Peace be unto you, my Lord King. May Allah's blessing rise about you. With your permission, O Ruler of the faithful, even a blunt sword in a weak hand can smite the enemy hip and thigh. The King looked at me and said: Ebrahim Bey, Take your hosts and go to wage war against the unbelievers, do not spare them and have no pity upon them and do not rest your head upon the pillow until you have destroyed them under the skies of my country. When I heard this, my heart began to sound like the voice of cornets while my eyes flashed like swords. I set my hand to my eyes and heart and fell to my knees again and said: Allah's shelter and Allah's messenger come to our Lord the King, as Allah hath said

and His emissary and the emissary of His emissary, so shall
Ebrahim your servant perform and do, O Ruler of all the Faithful.
The King gave me his blessing, may Allah's blessing rest upon
him, and suffered me to depart in peace. Ere the sun had reached
the West all we valiant men had gathered together and set out to
make war against the foe.

The battlefield was on the flanks of the desert. We had all that
we required of water and food, horses and camels, asses and
mules, swords and lances and bows, and all the other instruments
of war, so that the desert gleamed with them; and we came to do
battle against the foe.

The foe appeared before us with all kinds of weapons. All the
instruments of Satan were in his hands. Now the foe was stronger
and now we held sway, and it was almost certain that they would
fall into our hands.

But the unbelievers fought bravely for their lives. Some reeled
and fell and some rose refreshed, and the war was great and bitter.
Swords and lances flashed and iron clashed with iron, lopped
heads went spinning while hacked arms flew far and wide, man
and beast were trodden underfoot and the whole earth was flowing with blood. The legs of the beasts slipped and they fell away
under their riders, they were blinded by the blood of the corpses
and went crazy, while the instruments of Satan roared and
shrieked and rent and slew. He who fell did not rise up, while he
who crouched down was crushed. At the last only vestiges of all
the hosts were left on either side.

But we did not turn away from the foes, nor did they turn
away from us. They gathered the remainder of their soldiers and
came against us in a torrent of rage, while we leapt towards them
in a fury of vengeance. The cavalry flung themselves against them
first, then came the infantry and all the other troops. There was a
vast slaughter on that day. Many fell by the sword and many were
swept away in that flood of fire and brimstone and lead. As for
those who fled from the fighting, we destroyed them and closed
the roads. In that way our armies became divided. Some remained
to guard the prisoners and bury the dead while others went forth
to destroy those who had fled to the mountains and the wilderness.

For three days we went on slaying. At length we reached a spot
we did not know. Our camels and our horses fell and the earth
began to give off a stench. The food and water-carriers were three
days' journey away from us. All we had with us were skins and canteens which did not contain much. The weapons of war were a
burden on the men and the skins and canteens did not contain

water. The day flamed like an oven and there was no shadow for any creature. Not in the heavens alone was the sun enkindled, but it made the whole earth below seethe likewise. If you raised your head you were burned. If you lowered your face you were scorched. Of the enemies of the faithful there was no vestige, some had been driven off stupefied while some lay as dead carcasses, and Allah alone knows their number, while their corpses and the carcasses of our beasts went on raising more and more of a stench.

As for us, our life was no life either. No food was left and our canteens contained only enough to moisten the mouth. We raised our eyes up. There were only sandhills and stonehills. We turned our faces to the ground. The whole earth was like white fire. There were no trees, there was no spring, no beast or bird. Apart from the desert thorns there was nothing that grew. These thorns are not fit to be eaten even by camels, but as for us, as soon as we saw them each one thrust his head into their midst and sucked at them as a Christian sucking at swine-flesh; until their thorns entered into our tongues which became like cactus leaves.

Then our spirits fell and we cursed the hour that had brought us thither, and we cried: Alas, whither have we come. If Allah does not provide us with water and food then we are lost. Let us pray before Him, for He may accept our prayer and deliver us from destruction. Thereupon we raised our eyes aloft and said: There is no God but Allah and Mohamed is the messenger of Allah. We removed the thorns from our tongues and pressed and embraced the empty water-skins and canteens so that they might give us water; but none came out. We bit the skins with our teeth but there was only air. March we could not, for we had lost the way. We took counsel and climbed up a lofty hill, in case Allah might reveal a spring or tree or plant to us from there.

Yet all the places which we saw were like the place from which we came. No tree grew, no spring gurgled, no bird flew, no kid bleated, hill was entwined with hill and wilderness. We flung away out weapons and sat down bitter of spirit. This sitting was worst of all. Our limbs grew rusty and our tongues shriveled like a water-skin whose waters have dried.

Have we anything to eat? I asked my comrades. Shriveled water-skins, they answered. Cook them, said I, and we shall eat them. So we set the butts of our weapons on fire and roasted the water-skins.

When the water-skins were at an end we roasted our boots. As there was nothing left we went downhill. Yet all our descent was like a man who leaves one desert for another. The sun reached the west and the day grew dark. We hoped for a refreshing breeze, night came but not refreshment or ease. The moon and stars stood weary in the firmament. The sand had not been cooled and an aimless wind was caught amid the hills. Nor was the night that followed any better. An aimless wind held sway all night long. There was no change whatsoever in the air. That night there was a great fury in out hearts. We had been hoping to moisten our lips at night with the dew and to cool our bones, yet it was as parched as the day. We gazed aloft, and it seemed as though the moon and the stars and the planets were suffering as we did.

The third watch came. Stars and planets sank down in the firmament and a light breeze began to blow. As soon as the sun came out this likewise heated up. At the last it partnered with the whirlwind. We hid our faces in the ground, wrapped up in our robes, and wept for ourselves because of the desert wind. I sat thus for as long as I sat, with my face to the ground and my eyes turned low. I, at whose glance vast hosts of soldiers had trembled, feared to raise my head against a grain of sand. They had been fine, those days when I had headed my men and all had feared my word. The days had been fine when I had been at home and my menservants and maidservants had stood about to serve me, one raising a glowing coal for the nargileh, and another fanning me, while the fountains in the garden sprayed their water round about like a diadem of dew.

I shook myself at length, rose to my feet and removed my coat, and raised my voice and said: Come on, stand up. But my words were like a voice falling in a graveyard. My companions all lay dead, and those who had not yet died were as good as dead.

Thereupon I also wished to die. I remembered all the treasures and delights of Time which had formerly assembled together on my behalf. Now all of a sudden I was deprived of everything and was giving up my soul in the heart of the desert where there was no water to cleanse the corpse nor sextons to bury me. I raised mine eyes aloft and said, There is no God save God, let Him do with me whatever has been decreed for me.

But the Angel of Death had no wish as yet to set his hands on that man who is now talking. While I was still mourning for my household who were left without a master and for my children whom I was rendering orphans, I heard a sigh and saw that several of my comrades were quivering and moving.

O my brethren, said I, Allah has left you so that you should not perish in the desert. Hold out a little longer and let us mount yonder hill. If our descent serves no purpose, it may be that our ascent will have some purpose.

In this way I stood between the living and the dead, now raising my voice, and now whispering to myself, in order not to disturb my comrades for I had already despaired of their arising; but
so that I should feel that I myself had not perished. At last I also
grew silent. My tongue still moved convulsively, but my lips were
silent.

Yet Allah brought the sound to the ears of my comrades. Little
by little, slowly and swayingly, several of them rose to their feet in
order to proceed.

Ere we departed we covered the dead with sand, may God's
mercies and blessing rest upon them and all the Faithful; and we
said the prayer for the dead over them. We had no water wherewith to wash their bodies. May Allah cleanse them of their transgressions and make their judgment and our own more easy.

That hill was steep and smooth. Even a flea would have
slipped and fallen. Ere we had reached the hilltop, my companions had fallen and rolled down and broke their limbs, so that
nothing was left of us save myself and three companions.

When we had reached the hilltop we stood looking down at
fields and vineyards, and date-palms, flocks and herds. Sweet
breezes were blowing and bringing the fine scent and fragrance of
spices and springs of water. I raised my eyes aloft and said: Blessed
is He who counseled my heart to ascend, all lauds and praise to
the Laudable and Praiseworthy who brought us hither. We have
only to go down and we are saved.

Yet the descent was twice as hard as the ascent. Even a person
who had not seen what befell our companions would have feared
lest he became but a heap of bones; and this most assuredly we
felt who had seen men rolling and falling down, some with broken
heads and some with smashed and broken limbs. And yet those
breezes bearing sweet scents restored our spirit for us until the desire of life returned to our soul.

Let us make ourselves legs, said I to my companions, and descend. If we get there alive it will be good; and if not, then better
fall in an inhabited place than in a desert. For if we perish amid
human beings they will bury us and if we perish in the desert then
birds of prey will consume us like the idolaters, may God curse
them, who leave their dead to the birds of the heavens. My companions at once agreed, saying, "You have spoken well." If we die
we shall die among human beings who will bury us, while if we live
we shall return to our own places in order to comfort our house-
holds and kiss our children. So each one took his soul in hand,
and we went down on our hands and feet. Within a few moments

we found ourselves standing in an inhabited place of gardens and groves, amid date-palms and other good trees and waving ears of corn and a countryside running with water. Yet it seemed as though all our toil had been only in order that we should fall below. For while we were standing there my comrades fell in their tracks, and I also fell without knowing whether I was alive or dead.

I lay there as long as I lay without the strength to move a limb, and assuredly unable to stand up. My eyes closed and my body began to make a hollow in the ground below like a man who digs himself a pit and the earth receives him and holds him entrapped. If this is death, thought I to myself, then there is nothing better. I wished to ask my companions, what do you feel? Yet there was a weariness within me which caused me not to open my mouth.

While I was lying I heard a little kid bleating from the pasture; not the blast of trumpets nor the sound of people roaring and trampling. My soul returned to me and I slept. It seemed to me that I had returned home from the war and found my household established and my children alive. I greeted them and they greeted me in return. I kissed them and said, All lauds and praises to the Most Laudable and Praiseworthy, here I am with you and I shall not depart from you again until my end comes and I arise to my fate. I sat tranquilly and comforted my household and begat children upon children, and Allah rejoiced my heart and satisfied my desires. Yet all my tranquillity did not last long. I heard the sound of warfare and forgot what must not be forgotten and forsook my household to go forth against the enemy. And there I went on slaying until I had raised up a whole hill of dead. While I was standing up to my knees in blood, the earth trembled as though the ground were opening its mouth to swallow me up. I realized that I had departed from the world and was being led away to Gehenna, to be taken down to the lowest hells. I reminded Him on High of the wars that I had waged against the Unbelievers and how many of them I had slain in order that I might achieve merit on the Day of Judgment and ease my transgressions for me; and I cried, God is God.

Ere I had said "and Mohamed is His messenger," two men came who were tall as cedars and the lances in their hands were like date-palms that support the sky. And then I knew that the noise had come only from the sound of their feet. If they have come for peace, said I to myself, they have come only at the command of the creator in order to deliver me from hunger and thirst. But if they have to do battle, then it is an honor for a brave man to perish at the hands of these warriors.

Yet Allah found his believers worthy to have the secrets of this world revealed to them, and gave us strength and courage to remain alive until He His own Lofty Self resolves to take back our souls. I raised my eyes aloft in wonder at His creatures, may He be exalted, but they bent down to us and opened a water jar and moistened my lips and asked me a question. When they saw that we had no strength they picked us up in their hands and took us to their places, a place of tents which was as large about as the compass of the streets of Damascus and Stambul. Then they asked us in a tongue that was your own tongue. I looked about and saw men wearing cut and dyed garments bearing all kinds of weapons. Then I knew that we were among the Bnei-Khaibar, who rule in all those parts and have no sultan over them save from their own midst, and who fear no kingdom save the Kingdom of Heaven. I blessed the Blessed Allah who had brought us to them, since a covenant had once been made of old between Mohammed the messenger of Allah and this tribe of Khaibar. If our companions had held out a little while they would have come hither with us and would have rejoiced their souls with those things that Allah has created in His world. But Allah the Exalted does good to His creatures according to His own loving-kindness, decreeing thus for this one and thus for that one. He had decreed that our companions should fall in the desert, but for us we had decreed that we should live and enjoy His goodness in this world.

While we were sitting they brought us water to drink which tasted like the morning dew upon the mountains. After we had drunk and given thanks to Him who hath created good springs wherewith to restore the souls of His Believers, they set coffee before us. Much coffee had I drunk in my life, but never in all my days had I drunk coffee such as this, although I have often sat with great emirs and he who is set over them, our Lord and ruler the Sultan, may God show him all due mercy. After we had sat a while they brought us a broth, not of the flesh of beast or fowl nor of fish or vermin but of green-stuff; for during those years that they dwell in the wilderness they do not put out their hands to slay any living animal but are sustained from the earth and the fruits thereof. At the last they prepared soft couches for us. We lay down to sleep and lay all that night and all the following day until the sun set and it became night and it was time to fall asleep again. Then they came and spread a table before us and set all kind of food upon it; today a little, tomorrow more, then after the morrow more and more till flesh grew about our bones and our strength returned. Likewise they clothed and shod us and gave each of us a headcloth and a girdle to set about our heads.

We spent two weeks with them in this way and I saw things beyond the telling of any tongue. Yet I wish to tell you a little of what I saw. They are as many as the sands of the desert, and are dressed in noble garments and wrapped in woolen shawls with fringes and ride upon horses as befits the noble. Their neighbors are subject to them and pay them taxes, yet they hold their neighbors only in the way that the awe of a man is felt within his household. And every one of them is a warrior that is worth ten warriors. There are some among them who can take an Arab in hand as he rides on horseback and fling them both aloft, flinging the horse and receiving the Arab, without either of them touching the ground. When it is daytime each man goes to his field and vineyard and dates and cattle. When it is night he comes and sits down before the elders to hearken to the Torah of Moses your master. And their wives and daughters sit in their tents and cook and bake and milk the cattle and prepare buttermilk and cheese and spin and weave and sew and roll out bread and do not show their faces without, in order that men might not be led to ill thoughts on their account; for Allah has adorned their limbs and parts more than all women and has made them boundlessly beautiful and full of grace. There are women whose bodies are beautiful yet who have no charm and there are women with charm whose bodies are not beautiful. Yet among them the bodies are beautiful and the charm is also great. Some of them are like the sun in its radiance, for whosoever gazes at them is dazzled, and some are like the moon at its full, for whoever gazes at them becomes moonstruck. They do not cover their faces as our women do, for Allah has fashioned them a veil of honor and modesty, and no man looks upon them save their husbands. Each one of them rises early in the morning for prayer and they pray three times a day; and while they pray they turn their faces to Jerusalem. And on the Sabbath they do not leave their tents, but sit night and day praising His Lofty Name who has given them Sabbaths for rest. And they add part of the weekday to the Sabbath, both before and after. And ere the Sabbath begins they take off their weekly clothes and put down their weapons because the Sabbath protects them; and they put on golden array and light oil lamps, two for each; but in their tent of prayer they light twelve lamps, and they welcome the Sabbath as a man who welcomes the King to his home, and they make feasts in honor of it, singing songs and praises at each of these feasts. At the first feast they mention the name of Abraham, may he rest in peace, at the second the name of Isaac, may he rest in peace, and at the third the name of Jacob, may he rest in peace. And at the Sabbath close they all gather together and eat and drink and rejoice, bringing a gold chair and a large golden crown set with jewels and precious stones; and on the seat they set an elder garbed in finest pure gold array with sixty warriors running before him and sixty warriors running behind. And they shout and blow their trumpets and play their musical instruments and cry, "David, King of Israel, lives for ever." Thereupon all Israel come out of their tents at once and respond after them, "David, King of Israel, lives for ever," while all the women peep out at them from the apertures of the tents, and he claps his hands together and says "Kinghood is the Lord's." At this two elders come forth, one fetching him a staff and another a wallet. Then he descends from his throne and enters the sheepfolds where he feeds the kids and the goats. And he removes the royal robe from about him and the crown from on his head, and swathes himself in his shawl and goes to the elders and says: "My masters, I come but to learn." Thereupon the warriors put down their swords and put on their weekly clothes and go forth to their work. One goes to his field and one to his vineyard and dates, and one to his flocks and cattle, until God brings the Sabbath back to them.

In this way we dwelt with the Bnei-Khaibar and saw their strength and bravery and righteousness and generosity and loving-kindness, so that I forgot the half of the wars and all my victories and honor and glory in the land of the Believers, and rejoiced to have been brought to these noble ones of the people of the God of Abraham. May the Blessed One bless His blessed with His blessings.

Yet you can forget everything except the roof of the house which you saw for the first time when your mother gave birth to you. Ere long the Master of Dreams came and showed me my home and the hole from which the smoke comes out, and I smelt the scent of food cooked there and desired them with the longing of a pregnant woman.

What befell me also befell my companions. Day by day they desired more greatly to return to their places and drink the waters of their wells and eat the buttermilk of their flocks and teach their children the good qualities which they had learnt in the land of Khaibar.

Allah looked into our hearts. One day He brought us to a certain tent more handsome than all the others, with three elders seated in it whose faces were bright and shining as the light that was created on the First Day. And their beards were like the hanging clusters of dates. We were in awe of them at once, and fell on our faces and kissed the dust at their feet and said, We are your slaves. I saw that they did not understand our tongue and I began

to talk every language that I knew. The elders shook their beards
and I knew that they would sooner hear the talk of beasts and animals and fowls than the tongues of the Unbelievers. Yet it could
be seen from their faces that they had nothing against us at heart.

When we saw this, the souls within us were enlarged and we
gave thanks to him who is worthy of all thanksgiving and we kissed
the dust at their feet again, and said, God's shelter to His warriors
and honor to His elders.

Ere the day was out they set us on swift camels and returned
us to our own places. It may be in three hours or in two hours or
in one hour that we covered a journey of many days. And they
parted from us in peace. God's shelter and His peace be upon
them.

I entered my home and said, Peace be with you, my children.
But my greeting was orphaned. Ere I had come my children had
departed and had not returned. Likewise my friends did not come
to greet me. My sons and brothers had had the one fate. Both
alike had perished in the war. Likewise our Lord the Sultan had
returned his spirit to the God of Spirits. Likewise the kings who
had waged war against him had died, some of them at their own
hands and some at the hands of others. Time had not ended but
kings had come to an end. Yet that cry "David, King of Israel, lives
for ever" still resounds within my ears. Sometimes it is like a flaming fire and sometimes it is as sweet as the shadow of a date-palm.

I know for whom Eretz-Israel is set in store. It is intended only
for Israel. Yet for whom of Israel—those unto whom the Exalted
Creator gave magnificence and honor and strength and bravery
and generosity and loving kindness and who do His Exalted Will
out of love, they are the ones who will take over the rule therein
in the future. And their rule and kinghood will continue for ever
and ever.

I rose to my feet and said: Blessed be the Lord God of Israel
who permitted you to see what you have seen. Happy are we that
you too know for whom Eretz-Israel is intended. It was good for
Israel to safeguard their Torah, and esteem it above all things in
the land of which it is written, "And ye shall inherit it and ye shall
dwell therein and shall observe to do all the statutes"; save that
the day is short and the work is plentiful.

The All-and-Ever-Present has imposed many labors upon us.
We must plough and sow and harvest and set up sheaves and
thresh and winnow, and plant and hoe and pick the vintage and
tread the grapes, and prune the tree and beat the olives, we must
feed beasts and fowl and shear the sheep and watch over our soil

and labor against the destroyers and the thieves. Yet dwelling in
the land of Israel is a great deed which weighs against all the
commandments of the Torah. I am now going to take these plants
on my shoulder in order to plant them in our land, as it is written,
"And they shall plant vineyards and drink their wine and they shall
make gardens and eat the fruits thereof and I shall plant them on
their land and they shall never more be plucked away from their
land which I have given them, saith the Lord thy God." The Holy
and Blessed One has made His planting dependent upon our
planting. If we engage in our planting, then it is certain and sure
that the planting of the Holy and Blessed One will last and continue. The whole world is the Holy and Blessed One's, and He has
shared it out to His creatures according to His will. Esau and Ish-
mael have taken the fullness of the world and slay one another
and destroy one another for the kinghood which they would seize.
But we have received this little land from His blessed hand. We
have not come to seize kinghood or to hold dominion in it, but to
plough and sow and plant.

The pasha did not understand all I had said. He had spent but
a little time with the Jews of Khaibar and had not had opportunity
to learn much. Yet from his face it was plain that my words seemed
reasonable to him.

And so we sat as long as we sat, until day declined and the
evening breeze began to blow. The pasha rose and bade me
farewell in peace.

As he was about to turn away from me he looked at my sapling
and asked: In how many years will it bear fruit?

I told him.

He sighed and said: I shall not eat of it, but you and your children and your children's children will eat of them.

By the grace of the Holy and Blessed One, said I, looking
upwards.

(1941)

—Translated by I. M. Lask

From Foe to Friend

୭

Shmuel Yosef Agnon

Before Talpiot was built the King of the Winds used to rule over the entire region; and all his ministers and servants, mighty and stubborn winds, dwelled there with him and blew over mountain and valley, hill and ravine, doing whatever their hearts desired, as if the land had been given to them alone.

I went out there once and saw how lovely the place was—the air crisp, the sky pure blue, the land so open and free—and I strolled around a bit. A wind accosted me. "What are you doing here?" he said to me. "I'm taking a walk," I said. "Ah, you're taking a walk?" he said. He clapped me on the head and sent my hat flying. I bent down to pick it up. He rumpled my coat, turned it upside down over my head, and made a fool of me. I pulled my coat back off my head. He came at me again, knocked me to the ground and roared with wild laughter. I got to my feet and stood straight. He bumped up against me and shouted: "On your way! On your way!"

I saw I couldn't contend with one mightier than myself, and I went on my way.

I returned to the city and went inside my house. I became restless and went out. Whether I intended it or not, my feet carried me to Talpiot, I remembered all that the wind had done to me, I took some canvas and pegs and pitched a tent for myself—a refuge from wind and storm.

One night I stayed there. The light suddenly went out. I left the tent to see who had put my light out. I found the wind standing outside. "What do you want?" I asked him. He boxed my ears and slapped my mouth. I went back into my tent. He pulled up my tent pegs and split my rope, turned my tent over and ripped my canvas to shreds. He turned upon me as well, and almost knocked me over.

53

I saw I couldn't possibly match his strength. I picked up my feet and went back to the city.

I went back to the city and remained within its walls. I became restless and yearned for some place with fresh, pleasant air. Since there is no air anywhere in the entire land like the air of Talpiot, I went to Talpiot. And so that the wind wouldn't abuse me, I took some boards with me and made myself a hut. I thought I had found myself a resting-place, but the wind thought otherwise. A day hardly passed before he started thumping on my roof and shaking the walls. One night he carried off the whole hut.

The wind carried off my hut and left me without any shelter. I picked myself up and went back to the city.

What happened to me once and then a second time happened to me a third time. I returned to the city and I had no peace. How my heart drew me to that very spot from which I had been driven out!

I said to my heart: "Don't you see that it is impossible for us to return to a place from which we have been chased away? And what is impossible is impossible." But my heart thought differently. If I said a thousand times, *Impossible!* My heart replied a thousand and one times, "It *is* possible!"

I took wood and stones and built myself a house.

I won't praise my house, for it was small; but I am not ashamed of it, even though there are bigger and better houses. My house was small, but there was room enough in my house for a man like me who doesn't desire grandeur.

The wind saw that I had built myself a house. He came and asked me:

"What is this?"

"This is a house," I said to him.

He laughed and said: "I'll be damned if I ever saw anything as funny as this thing you call a house!"

I too laughed and said: "What you have never seen before, you see before you now."

He laughed and said: "What is it, this house?"

I laughed and said: "A house is . . . a house!"

He laughed and said to me: "I'll go and inspect it."

He stretched out his hand and inspected the door. The door broke and fell. He stretched out his hand and inspected the windows. The windows broke and fell. Finally he rose and went to the roof. Up he went and down came the roof. The wind laughed at me and said:

"Where is this house you built?"

I too asked where my house was. But I didn't laugh.

At first when the wind drove me away I used to return to the city. Finally things happened that prevented me from returning to the city. I was balked at every turn, and I didn't know what to do. To return to the city was impossible because of what had happened there; to return to Talpiot was impossible because of the wind who drove me out. I had made myself a tent and a hut, but they hadn't lasted. I had built myself a little house, but that hadn't stood up to the wind either. But then, maybe it hadn't withstood the wind because it was so small and frail; perhaps if it had been big and strong it would have stood. I took strong timber and sturdy beams, large blocks of stone, plaster and cement, and I hired good workers and watched over their work day and night. This time I was wise enough to sink the foundations very deep.

The house was built and it stood firm and upright on its own ground.

When the house was finished the wind came and thumped on the shutters.

"Who is rapping on my window?" I asked.

He laughed playfully and said: "A neighbor."

"What does one neighbor want of another on a night of storm and tempest like this?" I asked him.

He laughed and said: "He has come to wish his neighbor well in his new house."

"Is it usual for a neighbor to come through the window like a thief?" I said to him.

He came around and knocked on the door.

"Who is rapping on my door?" I said to him.

"It's I, your neighbor," said the wind.

"You are my neighbor—please come in," I said.

"But the door is locked," he said to me.

"Well, if the door is locked, it must be because I locked it," I said to him.

"Open up!" the wind answered.

"I'm sensitive to the cold; wait till the sun comes up and I will let you in," I said.

When the sun rose I went out to let him in but I couldn't find him. I stood in front of my house and saw that the land was desolate all around: not a tree, not a green leaf anywhere; only dust and stones. "I'll plant a garden here," I said to myself.

I took a spade and started digging. When the soil was ready I brought some saplings. The rains came and watered the saplings;

the dews came, and the saplings sprouted; the sun nourished them, and they blossomed. Not many days passed before the saplings that I had planted became trees with many branches.

I made myself a bench and sat in the shade of the trees.

One night the wind returned and started knocking the trees about. What did the trees do? They struck back at him. The wind rose again and shook the trees. Once more the trees struck in return. The wind lost his breath. He turned and went away.

From that time on the wind has been quite humble and meek, and when he comes he behaves like a gentleman. And since he minds his manners with me, I too mind my manners with him. When he comes I go out to meet him and ask him to sit with me on the garden bench beneath the trees. And he comes and sits by my side. And when he comes he brings with him a pleasant scent from the mountains and valleys, and he blows the air around me gently like a fan. Since he behaves like a complete penitent, I never remind him of his former deeds. And when he leaves me and goes on his way I invite him to come again, as one should with a good neighbor. And we really are the best of neighbors, and I am very fond of him. And he may even be fond of me.

(1941)

—Translated by Joel Blocker

The Prisoner

✧

S. YIZHAR

Shepherds and their flocks were scattered on the rocky hillsides, among the woods of low terebinth and the stretches of wild rose, and even along the swirling contours of valleys foaming with light, with those golden-green sparks of rustling summer grain under which the clodded earth, smelling of ancient soil, ripe and good, crumbles to gray flour at a foot's touch; on the plains and in the valleys flocks of sheep were wandering; on the hilltops, dim, human forms, one here and one there, sheltered in the shade of olive trees; it was clear that we could not advance without arousing excitement and destroying the purpose of our patrol.

We sat down on the rocks to rest a bit and to cool our dripping sweat in the sunlight. Everything hummed of summer, like a golden beehive. A whirlpool of gleaming mountain-fields, olive hills, and a sky ablaze with an intense silence blinded us for moments and so beguiled our hearts that one longed for a word of redeeming joy. And yet in the midst of the distant fields shepherds were calmly leading their flocks with the tranquil grace of fields and mountains and a kind of easy unconcern—the unconcern of good days when there was yet no evil in the world to forewarn of other evil things to come. In the distance quiet flocks were grazing, flocks from the days of Abraham, Isaac, and Jacob. A far-off village, wreathed with olive trees of dull copper, was slumbering in the curves of hills gathered like sheep against the mountains. But designs of a different sort cast their diagonal shadows across the pastoral scene!

For a long time our sergeant had been carefully peering through his field glasses, sucking his cigarette, and weaving plans. There was no point in going further, but to return empty-handed was out of the question. One of the shepherds, or at least one of their boys, or maybe several of them, had to be caught. Some action had to be taken, or something be burned. Then we could return with something concrete to point to, something accomplished.

The sergeant, of medium height, had thick brows which met over his deep-sunken eyes; his cap, pushed back on his balding head, exposed a receding forehead and damp, limp wisps of hair to the wind. We followed his gaze. Whatever it was that he saw, we saw a world of green-wool hills, a wasteland of boulders, and far-off olive trees, a world crisscrossed with golden valleys of grain— the kind of world that fills you with peace, while a lust for good, fertile earth urged one to return to back-bending work, to gray dust, to the toil of the burning summer: not to be one of the squad which the sergeant was planning to thrust bravely into the calm of the afternoon.

And, in fact, he was about ready to take action because just then we noticed a shepherd and his flock resting in the leveled grain in the shadow of a young, green oak. Instantly a circle was described in the world: outside the circle, everything else; inside, one man, isolated, to be hunted alive. And the hunters were already off. Most of the platoon took cover in the thickets and rocks to the right, while the sergeant and two or three others made an encircling movement down to the left in order to surprise their prey and drive him into the arms of the ambush above. Amidst the tender, golden grain we stole like thieves, trampling the bushes which the sheep had cropped so closely, our hobnails harshly kissing the warm, gray, sandy soil. We "took advantage" of the "terrain," of the "vegetation," of the protection offered by "natural cover," and we burst into a gallop toward the man seated on a rock in the shadow of the oak. Panic-stricken, he jumped to his feet, threw down his staff, lurched forward senselessly like a trapped gazelle, and disappeared over the top of the ridge right into the arms of his hunters.

What a laugh! What fun! Our sergeant hadn't recovered before another bright idea struck him, astonishingly bold and shrewd: take the sheep too! A complete operation! Drunk with satisfaction, he slapped one palm against the other and then rubbed them together as if to say, "This will be the real thing!" Someone else, smacking his lips, said: "Boy, what a stew that will be, I'm telling you . . ." And we willingly turned to the task, roused to a genuine enthusiasm by the flush of victory and the prospect of reward. "Come on! Let's get going!"

But the noise frightened the sheep. Some tossed their heads, some tried to flee, others waited to see what the rest would do. But who knew anything about handling sheep? We were ridiculous and that's just what our sergeant said, and he claimed that "schlemiels" and idiots like us could only mess up a good thing. Raising his voice, he began calling the sheep with a br-r-r and gr-r-r and a ta-ah-ta-ah and all the other noises and signs used by shepherds and their flocks from the beginning of time. He told one of the men to get in front of the sheep and to bleat, while some of us paired off on either side, brandishing our rifles like staffs and striking up a shepherd's tune, and three or more brought up the rear the same way. Thus, with a show of energy and wild laughter, we might overcome our hesitation, and be, in fact, soldiers.

In the confusion we had forgotten that behind a rock on the slope, huddled between two rifle butts and two pairs of spiked boots, sat our prisoner shivering like a rabbit—a man of about forty, with a moustache drooping at the corners of his mouth, a silly nose, slightly gaping lips, and eyes . . . but these were bound with his *kaffiyah* so that he couldn't see, although what he might have seen I don't know.

"Stand up," he was told as our sergeant came over to take a good look at the prisoner. "So you thought we wouldn't get a thing?" crowed the men. "We did, and how! With us there's no fooling around! Didn't have to waste a bullet: 'Hands up'—he got the idea right away."

"You're terrific," agreed the sergeant. "Just imagine: the shepherd *and* his flock! What won't they say when we get back! It's really great!" Only then did he look at the prisoner: a little man in a faded, yellow robe, breathing heavily behind the cloth over his eyes, his battered sandals like the flesh of his hooflike feet. On his hunched shoulders sat doom.

"Lift the blindfold, but tie his hands behind him. He'll lead the sheep for us." It was one of those crack commands which the intoxication of battle always inspired in our sergeant, and a spark of joy passed among us. Good. The men unwound the black cord of the shepherd's *kaffiyah,* took his hands and bound them with it good and tight, and then good and tight again for safety's sake, and still again for the third time. Then the blindfold was pushed above the nose of the frightened man: *"Nabi el ranam kudmana!"* he was ordered. "Lead the sheep ahead of us!"

I don't know what our prisoner thought upon seeing daylight again, what he felt in his heart, whether his blood whispered or roared, or what stirred helplessly in him. I don't know—but he immediately began clucking and grunting to his sheep as if nothing at all had happened, dropping from rock to rock through the brush with accustomed ease, the bewildered animals behind him. We followed after with hoarse yells, our rifles slapping our backs as we stampeded along and descended with wanton abandon to the valley.

We were so absorbed that we did not notice the silhouettes of other shepherds on the ridges of the hills, now gathering silently to peer at us from the distance as they rounded up their flocks; nor had we looked at the sun which all this busy hour had slipped lower and lower, getting more golden, until, turning the corner of a steep slope, we were struck by an intense blinding light: the smoky, enflamed disc seemed a mute admonition from space! But, of course, we had no time for all that: the flock! The prisoner! The sheep were bleating and scattering in all directions, while he seemed to shrivel up within himself, dazed and stupefied, his mind a ruin in which everything behind him was loss and all before him, despair. And as he walked he grew quieter, sadder, and more confused and bewildered.

It's too long to tell in detail how we made our way through valleys and past hills in the peaceful ripeness of summer; how the frightened sheep kept tripping over their own feet; how our prisoner was enveloped by dumbness, the silence of an uprooted plant—his misery so palpable that it flapped about his head in a rhythm of terror, rising and falling with the blindfold (tied to his brow with a brute twist of disdain) so that he was pathetic but also ludicrous and repulsive; how the grain turned more golden in the splendor of the sun; how the sandy paths followed their course between hills and fields with the faithful resignation of beasts of burden.

We were nearing our base of operations.

Signs of the base, and empty Arab village, became more frequent. Interrupted echoes. An abandoned anthill. The stench of desertion, the rot of humanity, infested, louse-ridden. The poverty and stupefaction of wretched villagers. The tatters of human existence. A sudden exposure of the limits of their homes, their yards, and of all within. They were revealed in their nakedness, impoverished, shriveled, and stinking. Sudden emptiness. Death by apoplexy. Strangeness, hostility, bereavement. An air of mourning—or was it boredom?—hovered there in the heat of the day. Whichever, it doesn't matter!

On the rim of the village, in those gray, greasy trenches, the other citizen-soldiers of our Home Guard company wandered aimlessly—their food no food, their water no water, their day no day and their night no night, saying to hell with what we'll do and to hell with what will be, to hell with everything that was once nice and comfortable, to hell with it all! We'll be dirty, we'll grow beards, we'll brag, and our clothes, wet with sweat, will stick to our unwashed bodies, infested with ulcers. We'll shoot stray dogs and let their carcasses stink, we'll sit in the clinging dust, we'll sleep in the filth, and we won't give a damn! It doesn't matter!

Nearing the trenches, we walked with heads high, proud of our loot! We fell smartly into step, almost dancing along. The bleating sheep were milling about in confusion. The prisoner, whose eyes had been covered again, dragged his sandals with clumsy uncertainty as we good-naturedly railed at him. We were happy and satisfied. What an adventure! What a job! Sweaty we were, caked with dust, but soldiers, real men! As for our sergeant, he was beside himself. Imagine our reception, the uproar and berserk laughter that broke loose like a barrel bursting its hoops!

Someone, laughing and sweating profusely, pointing at the unseeing prisoner, approached our sergeant. "Is that the prisoner? Want to finish him off? Let me!"

Our sergeant gulped some water, wiped his sweat and, still grinning, said, "Sit down over there. It's none of your business." The circle which had formed around howled with laughter. The trenches, the trouble, the disorder, no leave, and all that—what were they compared to all this?

One man was taking pictures of the whole scene, and on his next leave he would develop them. And there was one who sneaked up behind the prisoner, waved his fist passionately in the air and then, shaking with laughter, reeled back into the crowd. And there was the one who didn't know if this was proper or not, if it was the decent thing to do, and his eyes darted about seeking the support of an answer, whatever it might be. And there was one who, while talking, grabbed the water jug, raised it high over his head, and swilled the liquid with bared teeth, signaling to his audience with the forefinger of his left hand to wait until the last drop had been drained for the end of his slick story. And there was one wearing an undershirt who, astonished and curious, exposed his rotten teeth; many dentists, a skinny shrew of a wife, sleepless nights, narrow, stuffy rooms, unemployment, and working for "the party" had aggravated his eternal query of "Nu, what will be?"

And there were some who had steady jobs, some who were on their way up in the world, some who were hopeless cases to begin with, and some who rushed to the movies and all the theaters and read the weekend supplements of two newspapers. And there were

some who knew long passages by heart from Horace and the
Prophet Isaiah and from Chaim Nachman Bialik and even from
Shakespeare; some who loved their children and their wives and
their slippers and the little gardens at the sides of their houses;
some who hated all forms of favoritism, insisted that each man
keep his proper place in line, and raised a hue and cry at the
slightest suspicion of discrimination; some whose inherent good
nature had been permanently soured by the thought of paying
rent and taxes; some who were not at all what they seemed and
some who were exactly what they seemed. There they all stood, in
a happy circle around the blindfolded prisoner, who at that very
moment extended a calloused hand (one never knows if it's dirty,
only that it's the hand of a peasant) and said to them: *"Fi cigara?"*
Have you a cigarette?

His rasping voice (as if a wall had begun to speak) at once
aroused applause from those with a sense of the ridiculous. Others,
outraged by such impudence, raised their fingers admonishingly.

Even if someone were moved to think about a cigarette, it all
ended in a different way—in military style. Two corporals and a
sergeant came over from headquarters, took the prisoner, and led
him away. Unable to see, he innocently leaned on the arm which
the corporal had just as innocently extended in support. He even
spoke a few words to guide the prisoner's groping steps. And there
was a moment when it seemed as if both of them were laboring together peacefully to overcome the things that hindered their way
and helped each other as if they went together, a man and another man, close together—until they had almost reached the
house, when the prisoner repeated: *"Fi cigara?"* These few syllables
immediately spoiled the whole thing. The corporal withdrew his
arm that had been interlocked with the prisoner's, raised his eye-
brows angrily and, almost offended, shook himself free. "Did you
ever see such a thing?"

It happened so suddenly that the sightless man stumbled and
tripped on the front step of the house, lost his balance and, almost falling, plunged headlong into the room. In a desperate effort to right himself, he sent a chair flying and collided with the
table. There he stood, helpless, clumsy, overwhelmed by the force
of his own violence and the fear of what was to come. His arms
dropped to his sides and he stood stupefied, resigned to his fate.

A group of officers, their faces frozen in severe formality, had
been ceremoniously seated at the table. But the prisoner's sudden
entrance completely upset their quiet preparations, disturbed the atmosphere, confused the sentry at the door, confused the corporals

and the sergeant; in short, everything had to be put back together again and grudgingly reorganized from the very beginning.

The officer sitting in the middle was tall and muscular, with stubby hair and a fierce face. On his left sat none other than our sergeant. One could see now that he was quite bald; the hair above his forehead was still dark but what little hair he had at the temples was turning gray. Perspiring freely, a crumpled cigarette in his mouth, he was the hero of the day and only at the beginning of his glorious adventures. Near the wall, conspicuously removed from the others, stood a pale young fellow glancing about through half-lowered lashes like someone quite convinced of a particular truth but curious to see by precisely what means it stands to be revealed.

"What is your name?" The tall officer began his interrogation abruptly but the prisoner, still stunned, paid no attention. The lips of the young fellow leaning against the wall puckered with assurance: this was just what he had expected.

"What is your name?" repeated the tall officer, drawing out the syllables.

"Who? Me?" The prisoner trembled and reached for his blindfold with a faltering hand. Halfway there, he dropped it, as if it had been singed by flame.

"Your name?" the officer asked a third time in a tone that emphasized his patience.

"Hasan," he rasped, bowing his head, frustrated by his blindness.

"Hasan what?"

"Hasan Ahmed," he answered, now on the right course, and his head nodded affirmatively.

"How old?"

"Oh, so-so. Don't know exactly." He twitched his shoulders and slid his palms together uncertainly, wanting to be of help.

"How old?"

"Don't know, my lord," he said, moving his thick lips. For some reason he chuckled and his drooping moustache performed a little caper. "Twenty, maybe thirty," he said, eager to cooperate.

"Well, what's going on in your village?" The tall officer spoke with a restraint which, more than it emphasized his calm, betrayed the coming storm—the restraint of an original, cunning deceit, a kind of slow circular descent that is followed by a sudden swoop to the heart, a strike at the jugular.

"In the village they are working, my lord." The prisoner sketched a picture of country life, sniffing the trouble that was to come.

"Working, you say? As usual?" The interrogator was moving in like a spider when a trembling thread of the web announces the prey.

"Yes, my lord." The fly had edged away from the intricate web.

It was clear he would lie at this point. He had to lie. It was his duty to lie, and we would catch him by his tongue, the dirty dog, and we would show him. And just as we understood that with these tactics he would reveal nothing, so we knew that this time he wouldn't fool us. Not us. It's his turn to talk!

"Who is in your village?" The hawk hovered over its prey.

"Eh?" The prisoner did not follow the question and licked his lips innocently, like an animal.

"Jews? English? French?" The interrogator continued his questions like a teacher setting out to trap a slow pupil.

"No, my lord, no Jews, only Arabs." He answered earnestly, with no hint of evasion. Once again, as if the danger were over, he tugged absent-mindedly at his blindfold. The interrogator was glancing about the room: take a good look! It's beginning. Just see how an expert does it!

"Are you married?" He was started on a new, oblique attack. "Any children? Where is your father? How many brothers? Where does your village get its drinking water?" He wove his delicate web painstakingly, and the prisoner struggled to satisfy him; he fumbled uselessly with his hands and made superfluous, meaningless gestures, bobbing his head and rolling his tongue, getting involved in petty details which threw him into confusion and annoyed his interrogators: some story about two daughters and a son, and how the son, neglected by his sisters, went out of the house and, as a result, fell sick and passed from the world. As he mumbled along, the prisoner innocently scratched his back ribs up and down, first with his thumb and then with a knot of four fingers, stammering as he tried to find the right words—he was unbearable.

There was a pause. The sentry shifted his weight from one foot to the other. From the expression on the face of the young fellow leaning against the wall and from the way our balding sergeant got up from the table, it was suddenly clear—not that the prisoner had nothing more to say, but that nothing would help but a beating.

"Listen here, Hasan," said the interrogator, "are there any Egyptians in your village?" (Now he'll talk! Now it's going to begin. Now he's sure to lie.)

"There are," answered the prisoner, so simply it was disappointing.

"There are," echoed the interrogator resentfully, like a man who has been paid in advance by his debtor. He lit a cigarette, deep in thought, contemplating his next move.

Our sergeant paced back and forth across the room, re-arranged his chair, tucked in his shirttails, and with evident dissatisfaction turned his back to us and stared out the window. The young fellow by the wall, looking very wise, was passing his hand downward over his face, pinching his nose at the end of each stroke. You have to know how to handle these situations!

"How many are there?"

"Oh, so-so. Not many." (Now he'll start lying. This is it. Time for a beating.)

"How many?"

"Ten, maybe fifteen, about that."

"Listen, you Hasan, you'd better tell the truth."

"It's the truth, my lord, all the truth."

"And don't lie."

"Yes, yes, my lord." His hands, outstretched in surprise, dropped to his sides.

"Don't think you can fool around with us," the tall interrogator burst out. He felt it was the right moment to say this. "How many soldiers are there?"

"Fifteen."

"That's a lie."

The bald sergeant turned to us from the window. His eyes were smiling. He was enjoying that last sweet moment of anticipating all the joy still to come. To prolong it, he lit the cigarette held in the corner of his tightly-pressed lips. The other five men in the room regarded one another with the same wide-eyed pleasure. The sentry at the door shifted his weight again.

"I swear, my lord, fifteen."

"No more?"

"The truth, no more."

"How do you know there are no more?" The interrogator intended to make clear that he was nobody's fool.

"No more."

"And if there are more?" (How can one answer such a question?)

"No more!"

Suddenly a clumsy kick from too short a distance landed on the man at an awkward angle. The unsuspecting prisoner staggered and collapsed upon the table with a loud exclamation, more of surprise than of pain. The whole scene suggested some kind of unfairly matched game rather than a cross-examination, something unexpected, unnatural.

"Now talk and see that you tell the truth!"

"My lord, I swear by my own eyes, I swear by Allah, fifteen."

The young man by the wall was afraid that so gross a lie might be believed. He held a long stick which he drew through his fingers with the grace of a knight drawing his sword. Then silently, significantly, he placed it on the table.

The barrage of questions continues without a break. The kicks landed like lightning, more naturally and freely, cool, deliberate, increasingly skillful. If at times they seemed unavailing, they nonetheless continued.

Because if you want the truth, beat him! If he lies, beat him! If he tells the truth (don't you believe it!) beat him so he won't lie later on! Beat him in case there is more to come. Beat him because you've got him at your feet! Just as a tree when shaken lets fall its ripest fruit, so a prisoner if you strike him yields his choicest truths. That's clear. And if someone doesn't agree, let him not argue. He's a defeatist, and you can't make wars with that kind. Have no mercy. Beat him! They have no mercy on you. Besides, a *goy* is used to blows.

Now they came to the question of machine guns in the village. A crucial point, this. Here you have to lay it on or you won't get anywhere. And if you don't, Jewish blood will be spilt, our own boys' blood, so this point must be completely clear. They questioned him again and again until it became nauseating, and they gained nothing but the certainty that he was lying. Then he was ordered to describe the village's fortifications. And there he got completely confused. He had difficulty with the description, the abstraction, the geometry, the mathematics. He tried to convince his questioners with gestures, freeing his arms from his sleeves and waving them about while he shuffled back and forth. But the cloth over his eyes reduced everything to a blur of confusion. It was clear to everyone in the room that all his talk was nothing but a tissue of lies.

"You're a liar," exclaimed the discouraged interrogator. "I can see in your eyes that you're lying." And he raised a menacing fist in front of the prisoner's blindfold.

This got nowhere. It had become boring. Everyone was fed up. The cross-examination blundered along, without enthusiasm, and the kicks fell listlessly. There was sudden surprise when the stick came whistling down on the prisoner's back, a disinterested, routine blow from an obedient hand.

OK. And now about the guns. The prisoner kept insisting that their barrels were no longer than the distance from his shoulder to his palm. He struck his left palm like a hatchet against his right shoulder and then against his wrist: from here to there. He beat himself incessantly, unstintingly, to remove any trace of doubt. Even then he was uncertain whether he had done enough or must continue, and around his mouth was the expression of a blind man who has lost his way.

The questions petered out. At the door the sentry, shifting his weight from one foot to the other, was looking up at the sky, possibly searching in the glimmering light for something that was not in the dirty, gloomy room. He feared that something terrible was about to take place. It was inevitable! Take the stinking beggar, they would tell him, and get rid of him!

"Well, that's that," said the interrogator, slumping back in his chair, eager to relax now that it was over. He stubbed his cigarette impatiently on the floor.

"I'd better finish him off," volunteered the sergeant, flicking his cigarette through the doorway with a quick snap of his forefinger.

"He's a complete moron," concluded one of the corporals.

"He needs someone who can handle him," said the young man by the wall, curling his lips in a sneer at this offense to truth.

The prisoner, sensing a respite, licked his thick lips, stuck out a thick hand, and said: "*Fi cigara?*" Of course nobody paid attention to the stupid fool. After waiting some time, the idiot dropped his hand and remained rooted to the spot, sighing softly to himself: Oh, Lord God.

Well, what now: to the village quarry or perhaps a little more torture to open his mouth? Was there any other way to get rid of him? Or . . . perhaps one could give him a cigarette and send him home. Get out and let's not see you again!

In the end someone telephoned somewhere and spoke to the captain himself, and it was decided to move the prisoner to another camp (at least three of the men in the room wrinkled their noses in disgust at this unfit procedure, so civilian, so equivocal), a place which specialized in interrogating prisoners and meted out to each just what he deserved. The sentry—who had been uneasy throughout the cross-examination without knowing what to do—went to get the dusty jeep and the driver on duty. The young man who came was griping, angry that he had been called out of turn. Not that he objected to leaving: it would be nice to get back to civilization for a while and to see some human faces, but it was the principle, the principle of the thing! Another soldier, charged with an order whose execution had been delayed for lack of transport,

took his place alongside the driver. Now he was assigned another
duty: accompany the prisoner! (Thus shall they go through the
streets of the town: the machine gun in front and the prisoner behind!) He sat and loaded his machine gun. With two jobs, the
trip—God forbid!—couldn't be counted as leave!

The prisoner was pushed and shoved like a bundle into the
jeep where the only place left for him was the floor. There he was
dropped, kneeling like an animal. In front of him were the two
soldiers and behind, the sentry whose pocket held the official
order, travel authorization, and other essential papers. The afternoon, begun long ago among mountains, oaks, and sheep, was
now drawing to a close. Who could foresee how it would end?

The jeep left the moldering village behind, passed the dry
riverbeds, and spurted ahead at great speed through the fields,
bouncing on all fours. Distant details of the landscape kept shifting to close view. It was good to sit and watch the fields now
bathed in a rosy light trailing small, golden clouds, a light that
seemed to envelop everything—all those things which are so important to you and me but mattered not at all to the driver and his
comrade in the front seat. They smoked and whistled and sang
"On Desert Sand a Brave Man Fell" and "Beautiful Green Eyes" in
turn. It was difficult to know what the man who lay on the floor on
the jeep was feeling because he was blind, stunned, and silent.

A cloud of dust, billowing up behind the jeep like a train of
smoke, caught the rosy light in its outlines. The uneven gullies
and shallow furrows of the fields made the husky jeep dance. The
fields stretched to infinity, abandoned to the twilight, to something distant and dreamlike.

Suddenly, a strange thought pierces one's mind: *The woman is
lost beyond a doubt.* And before there's time to wonder where the
thought came from, one understands, with the shock of lightning,
that here, right here, a verdict is being rapped out which is called
by so many different names, among them: fate.

Quick, escape this rotten mess! Join the harmonizing of the
other two up front or journey toward a far distance with the deepening twilight. But the circle of that unexpected thought grows
larger and larger: This man here at your feet, his life, his well-
being, his home, three souls, the whole fabric of life, have somehow found their way into the hollow of your hand, as though you
were a little god sitting in the jeep. The abducted man, the stolen
sheep, those souls in the mountain village—single, living strands
that can be joined or separated or tangled together inextricably—
suddenly, you are the master of their fate. You have only to will it,

to stop the jeep and let him go, and the verdict will be changed. But wait . . . wait . . .

An inner force stirs in the young man on the back seat of the jeep and cries out: Wait! Free the prisoner!

We'll stop the jeep right here in the gully. We'll let him out, free his eyes, face him towards the hills, point straight ahead, and we'll say: Go home, man, it's straight that way. Watch for the ridge! There are Jews there. See that they don't get you again. Now he takes to his heels and runs home. He returns home. It's that easy. Just think: the dreadful, oppressive waiting; the fate of a woman (an Arab woman!) and her children; the will-he-or-won't-he-come-back?; that what-will-become-of-me-now?—all would end well, one could breathe freely again, and the verdict would be a return to life. Come, young man, let's go and free him.

Why not? Who's preventing you? It's simple, decent, human. Stop the driver. This time no more lofty phrases about humanity; this time it's in your hands. This time it's not someone else's wickedness. This time it's an affair between you and your conscience. Let him go and you'll save him. This time the choice (that terrible and important choice of which we always spoke with awe) is in your two hands. This time you can't escape behind "I'm a soldier" or "It's an order" or "If they catch me, what will they do?" or even behind "What will my comrades say?" You are naked now, facing your duty, and it is only yours.

So stop, driver! Send the man away! No need for reasons. It is his right and your duty. If there is a reason for this war, it must show itself now. Man, man, be a man and send him home. Spit on all this conventional cruelty. Send him away! Turn your back on those screaming slogans that paved the way for such an outrage as this! Free him! Hallelujah! let the shepherd return to his wife and his home!

There is no other way. Years might pass before he is set free, by some magic, to return to the hills to look for his wife and family; meanwhile, they have become fugitives fleeing misery and disease—mere human dust. Who knows what can happen in this meanwhile, and where? Perhaps, in this meanwhile someone will decide to get rid of him, to finish him off for some reason or even for no reason at all.

Why don't you make the driver stop? It's your duty, a duty from which there is no escape. It's so clear that it's hard to wait for you to act. Here you must rise and act. Say a word to the driver. Tell him and his companion that this was the order. Tell them a story, tell them something—or don't even bother. Just let it happen. You are going to face the sentence, that's sure. Let him go!

(How can I? He's not mine. He's not in my hands. It's not true that I'm his master. I'm only a messenger and nothing more. Is it my fault? Am I responsible for the hard hearts of others?)

That's enough. That's a shameful escape. That's the way every son-of-a-bitch escapes from a fateful decision and hides himself behind "I have no choice," those filthy and shopworn words. Where is your honor? Where is this independence of thought you boast about? Where is freedom, hurrah for freedom, the love of freedom! Free him! And what's more, prepare to be sentenced for this "crime." It's an honor. Where are they now, all your words, your protests, your rebellions about pettiness, about oppression, about the ways to truth and freedom? Today is your day of payment. And you shall pay, my son. It's in your hands.

(I can't. I'm nothing but a messenger. What's more, there's a war, and this man is from the other side. Perhaps he is a victim of the intrigues of his people but, after all, I am forbidden and have not the power to free him. What would happen if we all started to set prisoners free? Who knows, maybe he really knows something important and only puts on that silly face.)

Is that what you really think? Is he a soldier? Did you catch him with a sword in his hands? Where did you find him? He's not a fighter; he's a miserable, stinking civilian. This capture is a lie—don't blind your eyes to that. It's a crime. You've questioned him, haven't you? Now set him free. Nobody can get anything more out of him. And are you willing to suppress the truth for one more detail? The truth is to free him—now!

(It's so difficult to decide. I don't dare. It's involved with so much that's unpleasant: talk to the driver, persuade his companion, face all the questions, get into a rotten mess, and all because of a good-for-nothing wretch named Hasan, and what's more, I'm not sure it's good to free him before he's been thoroughly questioned.)

Vanity! Someone with only a fraction of your feelings about truth and freedom would stop right here and send the man home and continue on his way, quickly forgetting the whole thing: short and simple, a man of action. And he wouldn't thank himself for being good! But you, with all your knowledge, arguments, proofs, and dreams, it's clear that you won't do it. You're a noble fellow, you'll meditate, enthuse, regret, reconsider, you'll be submerged in a sea of thoughts: oh, why didn't I do it? And you'll cast the bitterness of your unfulfilled existence over the whole world: the world is ugly, the world is brutal. So make up your mind, and do it this time. Stand up to the test. Do it!

(I feel sorry for him. It's a shame they picked me for the job. I would do it if I weren't afraid . . . I don't know of what. If only I were alone with him here. It's bothering me like a desire almost within reach, and I can't begin. When I think that I'll have to explain, get all involved, go to people and argue and prove and start justifying myself, I simply can't. What can I do?)

Listen, man! Can you actually think of weighing these pitiful trifles against another's life? How would you look at this thing if you were the one crouched on the floor of the jeep, if it were your wife waiting at home, and all was destroyed, scattered to the winds like the chaff of the wheat?

The prisoner has already said all he can say, told all he can tell. What more do you want? And even if he has lied a hundred times, who is he and what is he? He is only a miserable nothing, a subdued, shriveled creature, a mask wrapped in a cloth, someone shrunken and stooped like a worthless sack, frightened, dissolving into nothingness, for whom being kicked is second nature (kick him—he's an Arab; it means nothing to him). As for you, his little god, it's your duty to free him, even if he himself laughs at you, even if he (or someone else) sees it as a sign of weakness on your part, even if your friends make fun of you, if they try to restrain you, even if they bring you up for court-martial, for twenty court-martials! It's your duty to break free of this habitual swinishness. Let there be one person who is ready—even at the price of suffering—to get out of this heap of filth which was piling up in the days when we were good citizens and which is now the celebrated, the accepted, the official way of the world, embraced by those bearing the proud title "soldier." And all that was frowned upon is now freely allowed!

Oh, Hasan Ahmed, you with a wife named Halima or Fatima, you with two daughters, you whose sheep have been stolen and who has been brought God knows where one clear afternoon, who are you and what is your life, you who can cleanse from our hearts all this filth—may it rot forever in darkness!

Of course you won't free him. That's clear. Beautiful words! It's even not cowardliness—it's worse than that: you are a partner to the crime. You. Hiding behind a stinking what-can-I-do-it's-an-order. This time you have the choice, and it's at your disposal. It's a big day. It's a day of rebellion. It's the day when, at last, you have the choice in your hands. And you hold the power to decide. And you can return life to a man from whom it has been taken. Think it over. You can behave according to the dictates of your heart, of your love, of your own standard of truth, and—most important of all—of the freedom of man.

Free him! Be a man! Free him!

It's clear that nothing will happen. It was certain that you would evade it, that you would turn away your eyes. It's clear that all is lost. Too bad for you, prisoner, he does not have the strength to act.

And maybe, even yet . . . you, you right here, it will only take a minute: Driver, stop! Hey, Hasan, get out and go home! Do it! Speak! Stop them! Talk! Right now! This is the moment! You can become at last, you sufferer of many long, empty days, you can become a man, the kind of man you've always wanted to be . . .

The glimmering plain was a thin, bright foil; thousands of acres shone like a magic loaf. There were no riverbeds, no hills, no ascents or descents, no trees, no villages. Everything was spread out to form a single golden matrix, round and gleaming, strewn with moving pinpoints of light, a vast expanse stretching to infinity. And yet behind us (but no one is gazing there) in the misty evening coming over the mountains, there, maybe, there is a different feeling, a gnawing sadness, the sadness of "who-knows?," of shameful impotence, the "who-knows?" that is in the heart of a waiting woman, the "who-knows?" of fate, a single, very personal "who-knows?", and still another "who-knows?" belonging to us all, which will remain here among us, unanswered, long after the sun has set.

(1949)

—Translated by V. C. Rycus

The Swimming Race

∾

BENJAMIN TAMMUZ

I

One hot summer's day many years ago I was sitting in the kitchen at home, staring out of the window. The chill of the red floor tile seeped into my bare feet. With my elbows leaning on the oil-cloth-covered table, I let my eyes stray outside. The rooms were pervaded by the afternoon stillness and I felt dreamily at peace.

Suddenly, galloping hoofbeats sounded down the road and a black Arab horse-cab—the kind that plied the roads before cars took over—came into view; it was like those cabs we used to hire to drive us to the Jaffa railway station when we traveled up to Jerusalem to spend Passover with Grandmother.

The horses drew nearer and were reined in outside our house, and the Arab cabman alighted and knocked at our door. I jumped up to open it, and a musty smell filled the kitchen—a smell of horses and far-off places. The cabman's shoulders blocked out the light and prevented the sultry heat from forcing its way inside.

He handed me a letter. I glanced at it and saw it was in French, which I could not read. My mother entered and took the letter, and her face lit up. She asked the cabman in and placed a slice of cold watermelon and a fresh pita on the table before him. Leaning his whip against the wall, the Arab thanked her for her kindness, sat down at the table, and began taking large bites out of the watermelon, filling the air with the smacking of his lips.

My mother told me that the letter was from the old Arab woman who lived in the orange grove. She wrote that she was well again and her pains had left her, and that she had been cured by my mother's hands, which she kissed from afar. She also wrote that now that summer had come and she had heard our holidays

73

would soon be coming round, she hoped my mother would be able to get away from her other patients and come with her son to stay at her house in the orange grove.

The sun was about to sink into the sea as we left the house and climbed into the cab. The cabman folded back the rounded leather hood, and as we sank into the deep, soft seat I was instantly overwhelmed by a sensation of traveling to distant parts. The Arab climbed onto his high perch, whistled to his horses, and flicked his whip in the air. The springs creaked, the seat sank and surged up again beneath us like an ocean swell, and a farewell whinny rose on the air. With a wrench of wheels the cab moved off, its rumble over the pitted road sounding like a joyful melody.

Before long we had left the Hassan-Beq Mosque behind and were plunging through the alleyways of the Manshieh quarter. Smells of cooking assailed our nostrils: waves of *za'tar*, of roast mutton, of fried aubergine and mint-spiced salad washed over us in turn. The cabman's voice filled the air, sounding warnings right and left, coaxing street-hawkers to move out of our path, bawling out the urchins who squatted in the middle of the road. The horses trotted in a lively, unbroken rhythm, their brown shiny rumps swaying from side to side. The horse on the right, without breaking his stride, pricked up his tail and dropped his dung. Turning around on his lofty seat, the cabman threw us an apologetic smile and remarked that horses were shameless ill-bred creatures and we must excuse them.

We jogged along pleasurably and restfully in our seats till the city lay behind us and the horses were drawing the cab laboriously along the track of reddish sand lined with hedgerows of cactus and acacia. Waves of heat rose from the sand, settling beside us onto the cool seat. The sun must already have dipped into the sea, for beyond the orange groves the skies glowed crimson and a chilly dusk descended all around. Suddenly the horses stopped and made water on the sand in unison.

Again the cab lurched forward. A quiver rippled the horses' hides as their hooves struck a stretch of limestone-paved road, lined by cypresses on either side. Before us stood an archway of whitewashed stone, enclosing a large, closed wooden gate with a small wicket set in it. Near the wicket stood a girl of about my age, wearing a white frock and with a ribbon in her hair. As the cab drew up at the gate she bolted inside, and the cabman said, "We're there!"

You don't see such courtyards any more. And if you should happen to come to a place where there once was such a courtyard, you will only find a scene of wartime destruction: heaps of rubble and rafters, with cobwebs trying to impart an air of antiquity to what only yesterday still breathed and laughed.

But in those days the courtyard was in good repair and throbbing with life. It was square-shaped and enclosed on three sides by a two-story building, with stables and barns occupying the lower story. Black and red hens roamed about the yard, their clucking mingling with the neighing of horses. On the second floor was a pump house, and next to it a pool-like reservoir into which water splashed from a pipe leading from the pump. Goldfish gathered near the outlet, darting among the bubbles created by the jet of water. A wooden parapet railed in a long veranda that always lay in the shade. A colored glass door led from the veranda into a central reception room, from which numerous doors opened onto the living rooms, the kitchen, and the pantries.

In the center of the room stood a long table surrounded by upholstered armchairs. In anticipation of our arrival that day, their white linen dust covers had been removed and lay folded in neat piles in a corner. Earthenware vases painted red and gold were arranged about the room; they contained large paper roses and lilies, some of them fashioned into strange unflowerlike shapes. One vase, its paint long faded, had been brought there on the wedding day of the elderly mistress of the house.

From gilt wooden frames on the walls stared the portraits of sword-bearing men in fezzes. The old lady led my mother up to one of the pictures and said, "My husband, may he rest in peace! His father built this house. Now we live here during the summer and go back to Jaffa for the winter."

With a sigh my mother replied, "My husband's no longer alive, either. But his house and his father's house aren't here; everything remained over there, abroad, and I live in a rented apartment summer and winter."

"That's because you are newcomers, immigrants," the old lady said. "But with the help of God you'll thrive and build yourselves houses. You're hard-working people and your hands are blessed."

My mother caught the hint and threw her a grateful look, but I blurted out: "But it's not true that we're driving the Arabs out. We are out for peace, not war."

Placing her hand on my head, the old lady said, "It all depends on the individual; everyone who wants peace will live in peace."

At that moment the young girl appeared in the doorway.

"Come over here, Nahida," the old lady said, "and kiss the hand of the *hakima** who cured your grandmother. And this is her son."

Nahida came hesitantly into the room and stood in front of my mother. My mother embraced her and kissed her on the cheek, and a flush suffused the girl's dark complexion. She hung her head and remained silent.

"Our Nahida is shy," the old lady said, "but her heart is kind."

Hitching up her white skirt, Nahida sat down in an armchair. The rest of us sat down, too, as though permitted to do so now that the most honored person among us was seated.

The old lady made a remark in French and my mother laughed. Again Nahida blushed and I noticed her eyeing me to see whether I understood French.

"I don't understand a word," I told her. "What are they saying?"

"My grandmother says you and I would make a fine couple."

"Rubbish!" I answered and stared at the floor.

"You can go and play," the old woman said. "We're not keeping you."

I got up and followed Nahida out onto the veranda. We went and sat down at the edge of the pool.

"Do you believe in God?" I asked her. "Because I don't, not at all."

"I do, and I have a place in the grove where I go and pray. If we become friends I'll take you there and I'll show you there's a God."

"Then you fast in the month of Ramadan?" I asked. "I eat even on Yom-Kippur."

"I don't fast because I'm still too young. Do you rest on the Sabbath?"

"That depends," I answered. "I rest if I've got nothing else to do. Not because there's a God, but just if I feel like it."

"But I love God," Nahida said.

"Then we certainly won't make a couple unless you stop believing."

Nahida was about to make some retort when we heard the gate open, and two men entered the yard. Nahida leapt up and rushed over to them, throwing her arms around the neck of the older man, who wore a fez and European clothes.

"Daddy, we have visitors!" she cried.

*Woman doctor.

"I know," her father replied. "The *hakima* has come to see us."

I stood up and waited for them to mount the steps to the pool. The second man, who wore a *keffiyeh* and *agal* and looked about eighteen, was Nahida's uncle, her father's brother. He came up first and held out his hand to greet me. Nahida's father patted my cheek and ushered me into the house.

We had supper out on the veranda. We were served large dishes of fried potatoes, sliced aubergine in tomato sauce and diced salted cheese, and a bowl of pomegranates and watermelons. There was a heap of hot pitas in the center of the table.

Nahida's uncle—his name was Abdul-Karim—asked me if I was in the Haganah. When I told him that was a secret, he laughed and said it was an open secret which the whole country knew about.

"Abdul-Karim is studying at the College of the Mufti," Nahida's father told us. "And he's in constant fear of your Haganah."

Abdul-Karim's face darkened and he kept silent; but the old lady, his mother, laid her hand on his arm and said, "My Abdul-Karim is a fine, loyal man. Don't you tease him."

Abdul-Karim kissed his mother's hand and said nothing.

Just then, a shaggy sheepdog appeared on the veranda and wriggled under the table, butting against the tangle of legs as it looked for a spot to lie down. Finally it came to rest with its head on Nahida's feet and its tail on mine; it kept licking Nahida's feet, and its wagging tail tickled mine. The tickling made me smile and I turned to explain to Nahida why I was smiling, but when I saw she was taking my smile as a mark of friendship, I kept quiet.

When supper was over, Nahida's father said to his brother:

"Abdul-Karim my brother, go and show the children what you've brought from town."

Motioning to Nahida and myself to follow him, Abdul-Karim went into a toolshed in the orange grove and came out with a brand-new shotgun.

"We'll go hunting rabbits tomorrow," he said. "Know how to fire a gun?"

"A little," I told him. "We can have a shooting match if you like."

"We had a swimming match here in the pool last week," Nahida said, "and my uncle beat them all."

"*Ahlan u-sahlan!*"* Abdul-Karim agreed. "Tomorrow morning, then. Now let's get back to the house and listen to some songs. We have a gramophone."

*With pleasure.

Back in the house, Abdul-Karim put on a record, wound the handle, and adjusted the soundbox. The sound of a *kamanji* and drum and cymbals issued forth, immediately followed by an Arab song, sung in a sweet plaintive voice, with delicate, floating trills. Abdul-Karim sprawled back contentedly in his armchair, his face beaming.

When the record ended he put on another, though to me it seemed as though the same song was being played over again. This went on again and again till I got bored and slipped out to another room where my mother was chatting with the old lady. But that bored me too, so I went out to the veranda and gazed at the pool and the orange grove beyond. A large moon hung just above the treetops and a chill arose from the water in the pool. Some night bird was calling nearby, but stopped whenever the gramophone fell silent. As a yawn escaped me, I thought regretfully of my pals at home who were probably roasting potatoes on a fire under the electricity pylon, having pilfered the wood from the nearby sausage factory. What had made me come here? I asked myself.

Nahida found a queer way of waking me up next morning. They had a fat, lazy cat in the house, which Nahida dropped onto my face while I was asleep. I leapt out of bed and flung the cat back into her lap. That was how we started our second day in the house in the orange grove.

I was still brushing my teeth when Abdul-Karim came into the kitchen and said, "What about our swimming race?"

"I'm ready," I told him.

We hurried through breakfast, got into bathing trunks, and went outside. My mother, the old lady, and Nahida's father had already drawn up chairs at the side of the pool to watch the race.

"Ready, steady . . . go!" Nahida called out, and Abdul-Karim and I dived in. Either because I was overexcited or I wasn't used to fresh water, I sank to the bottom like a stone, and by the time I had recovered sufficiently to surface, Abdul-Karim was already halfway across. I saw my mother bending over the parapet and heard her calling out to me, "Don't be afraid! Swim fast!" I started swimming, but it was no use. By the time I reached the pipe leading from the pump house, Abdul-Karim was already sitting on the parapet on the far side, squeezing the water out of his hair.

"You beat me in the pool," I told him. "But I'll take you on at anything else, if you want."

"At what?" he asked.

"Let's say at arithmetic."

"Why not?" he answered, and told Nahida to fetch some paper and pencils. When Nahida came back with them, I tore a sheet of paper into two halves, and on each I wrote down seven million, nine hundred and eighty-four thousand, six hundred and ninety-eight multiplied by four million, nine hundred and eighty-six thousand, seven hundred and fifty-nine.

"Let's see who figures that out first," I said.

Taking a pencil, Abdul-Karim started jotting down figures, and so did I. I was through before he was and handed my sheet to Nahida's father to check. It turned out I had a mistake. Then Abdul-Karim handed over his paper and it turned out that he had gone wrong, too.

"Then let's have a general knowledge competition," I challenged Abdul-Karim. "For instance: who discovered America?"

"Columbus," Abdul-Karim answered.

"Wrong!" I said. "It was Amerigo Vespucci, and that's why it's called America!"

"He beat you!" Nahida called to her uncle. "You see, he beat you!"

"He beat me in America," Abdul-Carim said, "but I beat him *right here,* in the pool."

"You wait till I'm grown up and then I'll beat you right here in the pool," I told him.

Nahida seemed about to nod agreement, but thought better of it and looked at her uncle to see what he was going to answer to that.

"If he ever manages to beat me here in the pool," Abdul-Karim said, "it will be very bad indeed. It will be bad for you too, Nahida. Bad for all of us."

We didn't get his meaning and I wanted to tell him to cut out his philosophizing; but I didn't know how to say that in Arabic, so I kept quiet.

Later we went hunting rabbits in the orange grove.

II

Many years had gone by and summer had come round once again. Tired out after the year's work, I was looking for someplace where I could take a fortnight's rest. Packing a small valise, I traveled up to Jerusalem, only to find all the boarding houses full. Finally, wearied by rushing about the city, I boarded a bus bound for the Arab village of Ein-Karem. As I took my seat, I started wondering what I would do there and what had made me go there of all places.

At the end of the main street stood a domed building, with a fountain gushing out from under its floor. Opposite, on a hillside that sloped up to the Russian monastery on its summit, in the shade of a clump of sycamores, some men sat on low wooden stools, sipping coffee and puffing at their *narghiles*. I walked over and sat down on one of the stools, and when the waiter came over to take my order, I asked him if he knew of a family that would be willing to put me up for a couple of weeks.

"I don't know of one," the lad answered. "But maybe the owner does."

The café proprietor came over to have a look at me. "A family to put you up?" he said. "What for?"

"To take a rest," I answered. "I'm tired and I'm looking for somewhere to rest."

"And how much are you willing to pay?" he asked.

"As much as I have to," I replied.

The proprietor sent the lad to the house of a certain Abu-Nimr. Before long he came back and said:

"Go up that way. Abu-Nimr is willing."

Picking up my valise, I trudged up the hillside, wondering all the time what had made me come to this place. I entered a courtyard and knocked at the door of the house indicated. A tall, bald Arab of about forty-five came out and said, "Welcome! Come right in."

I let him precede me down a long, cool passage and into a small room, almost entirely taken up by a tall, wide bed.

"If you like it, you're welcome," Abu-Nimr said.

"It's very nice," I said. "How much will it cost?"

"I don't know. My wife will tell you that," he said and left the room.

I unpacked my valise and sat down on the bed, instantly sinking into the soft bedding, which billowed up to my elbows. There was a deep stillness all around, pervaded by the familiar smells of frying oil, mint leaves, black coffee, rosewater, and cardamum seeds. I felt my face break into a smile as my ears strained to catch a sound that was missing in order to complete a dim, distant memory.

Suddenly I heard a tap turned on in the kitchen and the sound of gushing water made me hold my breath: water gushing from a pipe into a pool!

I got up and went out to the yard. There was no pool, not even orange trees; but there was something about the apple and plum trees, some quality of strangeness peculiar to an Arab homestead. It was obvious that the courtyard had not evolved all at once, that each generation had added something of its own. One man had planted the apple tree by the water tap, another the mulberry tree near the dog kennel, and in time the garden had sprouted up to tell its masters' life stories. I stood listening, my fantasy peopling the courtyard with Nahida and her grandmother, with Abdul-Karim, with the horse-cab that would suddenly draw to a halt outside the gate and the horses that would stand and urinate.

That evening I was invited to join the family at supper, and Abu-Nimr introduced me to the people who sat round the table: his round-faced, bustling wife, who smiled into space without resting her eyes on me; his two sons, aged thirteen and fifteen, who attended high school in the city; his plump, white-skinned daughter, married to a policeman who was away from home all week, and who came home loaded with a wicker basket containing a trussed pigeon, apples from Betar, and a dozen eggs commandeered from some villager who happened to call at the police station.

The food that was served was no more than a continuation of that faraway supper in the orange grove. At that moment I realized what I had come there for.

After supper the strains of an Arab song arose from the gramophone. Abu-Nimr asked me whether I would care to show his boys how to operate the English typewriter he had bought in the city the day before. I sat down to instruct the lads, who set about their task with tremendous awe while their parents looked on, their hearts overflowing with pride. After a while their mother brought me a glass of cocoa and urged me to take a little rest. The gramophone was still playing, and as I sipped my drink Nahida's voice came back to me and Abdul-Karim's features formed themselves before my eyes, and out of the gloom in the passage there arose the sounds of my mother chatting with the old lady. It was then that I knew that I had been waiting all these years for just this moment, that I would relive our stay at the house in the orange grove.

III

Again the years went by. We were in the grip of war with the Arabs. I was serving in a company that was lined up to storm Tel-Arish, an Arab stronghold in the Jaffa dunes, east of the city.

We had launched an abortive attack there several weeks before which had cost us twenty-six men. This time we felt sure of success and looked forward to the battle as a fierce retaliation.

We set out from Holon at midnight, and soon began crawling in the direction of the Tel-Arish buildings. The sand dunes afforded excellent cover, and we slipped across them effortlessly and soundlessly. A west wind carried the Jaffa smells over to us, but later the wing veered round behind us, from the new estates going up in Holon, breathing the smell of new, white houses on our backs. The sand beneath us surrendered the sun's warmth it had absorbed during the day, telling of the days of light we had known among the white houses, and auguring the liberty and joy that would again be ours once victory had been gained.

When the Arabs spotted us it was too late for them to do anything about it. We were already within grenade range of their position, and we stormed it from three sides. One of the first grenades burst inside their forward machine-gun nest, putting all its crew out of action. We charged inside and raked the village with the German machine gun. The Arabs there panicked and rushed out of the houses, only to be cut down by our riflemen, who lay in ambush on our two flanks to the north and south. This left the Arabs only one escape route, westwards, and it appeared that some of them managed to slip through in that direction and escape into the cover of the nearby orange grove—the same grove were, about twenty years before, I had spent a few days with the old lady's family.

I had been expecting things to turn out like that, for that was how it had been planned. The house in the orange grove was our second objective that night. We didn't know whether there were any soldiers there, but we were quite sure that any we failed to destroy at the Tel-Arish position would easily be able to reorganize and entrench themselves in the stone building and courtyard. It seemed that they had kept a reserve force in the house in the orange grove, for heavy fire was opened upon us from that direction, and there were other indications that fortified positions there were ready to go into action in the event that Tel-Arish should fall.

Our luck didn't hold out there, however: the battle continued till dawn and we lost six men. This only heightened our desire for revenge, and besides, we still outnumbered them. Soon the defense of the house showed signs of weakening and the fire gradually slackened off. At dawn we rushed the courtyard, got through as far as the stables, and laid a charge of high explosives, then withdrew. A few moments later there was a violent clap of thunder and the wing of the house next to the pool collapsed into a heap of rubble. This was immediately followed by the groans of the

wounded and cries of surrender. We remustered in the courtyard
and shouted to the Arabs to come out and surrender.

I was not surprised to see Abdul-Karim. He seemed to have expected this, too, though that was something I had never dared to
imagine. I recognized him straight away. I went up to him and
called his name. When I explained who I was, he gave a weary
smile of recollection.

"Nahida . . . is she here too?" I asked him.

"No," he said. "The family has left Jaffa."

Some of the boys listened to our conversation in surprise.

"D'you know him?" our officer asked me.

"I know him," I said.

"Can he give us any important information?"

"Maybe," I said. "But let me settle an old score with him first."

"Want to finish him off?" the officer asked me.

"No," I told him. "I just want to talk to him."

The boys burst out laughing at this. Abdul-Karim, who hadn't
understood what we were saying, must have been insulted for his
hands trembled with suppressed fury.

I hastened to explain to him that I wanted to talk to him alone.

"You're the victors," he said. "We do as we're told."

"As long as I haven't beaten you in the pool," I told him,
"there's no telling who is the victor."

Abdul-Karim smiled. He seemed to have got my meaning.

Our officer didn't seem to get it, however, for he ordered
Abdul-Karim to be taken into the orange grove, where the prisoners were being rounded up. I went up to the pool and sat down on
the parapet. Our reinforcements from Bat-Yam and Holon began
to appear and the orderlies set about attending to the wounded in
the courtyard. I stripped and entered the water. It was warm and
dirty: it must have been a long time since the pipe overhead had
jetted water from the well pump.

Stretching out my arms, I swam across the pool, then back
again. I closed my eyes and waited to hear my mother's voice, urg-
ing me on: "Don't be scared! Swim fast!" But instead, I heard
Abdul-Karim say: "You beat me in America, but I beat you *right
here*, in the pool."

Just then I heard a shot from the orange grove. My heart
missed a beat. I knew Abdul-Karim had been killed.

Leaping out of the water, I pulled on my trousers and rushed
into the grove. There was commotion and the officer was yelling:

"Who the hell fired that shot?"

"My gun went off," one of the boys said.

When he saw me coming up the officer said, "We've lost that information, damn it! They've killed that Arab of yours."

"We've lost it," I said.

I went over to Abdul-Karim's body and turned it over. He looked as though he had seen me swimming in the pool a few moments ago. His was not the expression of a man who had lost.

There, in the courtyard, it was I, all of us, who were the losers.

(1951)

—Translated by Joseph Schachter

Facing the Forests

❧

A. B. YEHOSHUA

Another winter lost in fog. As usual he did nothing; postponed examinations, left papers unwritten. He had completed all his courses long ago, attended all the lectures, and the string of signatures on his tattered student card testified that all had fulfilled their duty, silently disappeared, and left the rest of the task in his own limp hands. But words weary him; his own, let alone the words of others. He drifts from one rented room to another, rootless, jobless. But for an occasional job tutoring backward children he would starve to death. Here he is approaching thirty and a bald spot crowns his wilting head. His defective eyesight blurs many things. His dreams at night are dull. They are uneventful; a yellow waste, where a few stunted trees may spring up in a moment of grace, and a naked woman. At student revels he is already looked at with faint ridicule. The speed with which he gets drunk is a regular part of the program. He never misses a party. They need him still. His limp figure is extremely popular and there is no one like him for bridging gaps between people. His erstwhile fellow students have since graduated and may be seen carrying bulging briefcases, on their way to work every morning of the week. Sometimes, at noon, returning from their office, they may encounter him in the street with his just-awake eyes: a gray moth in search of its first meal. They, having heard of his dissipations, promptly pronounce the unanimous, half-pitying half-exasperated decree: "Solitude!"

Solitude is what he needs. For he is not without talent nor does he lack brains. He needs to strengthen his will power.

He, as a rule, will drop his arms by his sides in a gesture of pious despair, back up against the nearest available wall, languidly cross his legs and plead in a whisper: "But where? Go on, tell me, where?"

For look, he himself is craving solitude. He plainly needs to renew his acquaintance with words, to try to concentrate on the material that threatens ever to wear him down. But then he would have to enter prison. He knows himself (a sickly smile): if there should be the tiniest crack through he would make it a tunnel of escape at once. No, please, no favors. Either—or.

Some content themselves with this feeble excuse, shrug their shoulders wryly, and go their way. But his real friends, those whose wives he loves as well, two budding lecturers who remember him from days gone by, remember him favorably for the two or three amazingly original ideas that he had dropped at random during his student days—friends who are concerned for his future—these two are well aware that the coming spring is that much more dangerous to him, that his desultory affairs with women will but draw zeal from the blue skies. Is it any wonder then if one fine day they will catch hold of him in the street, their eyes sparkling. "Well, your lordship, we've found the solution to your lordship's problem at last." And he will be quick to show an expectant eagerness, though cunning enough to leave himself ample means of retreat.

"What?"

The function of forest scout. A fire watcher. Yes, it's something new. A dream of a job, a plum. Utter, profound solitude. There he will be able to scrape together his crumbled existence.

Where did they get the idea?

From the papers, yes, from a casual skimming of the daily papers.

He is astonished, laughs inordinately, hysterically almost. What now? What's the idea? Forests . . . What forests? Since when do we have forests in this country? What do they mean?

But they refuse to smile. For once they are determined. Before he has time to digest their words they have burned the bridges over which he had meant to escape, as usual. "You said, either—or. Here is your solution."

He glances at his watch, pretending haste. Will not a single spark light up in him then? For he, too, loathes himself, doesn't he?

And so, when spring has set the windows ajar he arrives early one morning at the Afforestation Department. A sunny office, a clerk, a typist, several typists. He enters quickly, armed with impressive recommendations, heralded by telephone calls. The man in charge

of the forests, a worthy character edging his way to old age, is
faintly amused (his position permits him as much), grins to himself. Much ado about nothing, about such a marginal job. Hence
he is curious about the caller, considers rising to receive him,
even. The plain patch of wilderness on top of the head of the candidate adds to his stature. The fellow inspires trust, surely, is surely
meant for better things.

"Are you certain that this is what you want? The observation
post is a grim place. Only really primitive people can bear such
solitude. What is it you wish to write? Your doctorate?"

No, sad to say, he is still at the elementary stages of his study.

Yes, he has wasted much time.

No, he has no family.

Yes, with glasses his vision was sound.

Gently the old manager explains that, in accordance with a
certain semi-official agreement, this work is reserved for social
cases only and not for how-shall-I-put-it, romantics, ha-ha, intellectuals in search of solitude . . . However, he is prepared, just this
once, to make an exception and include an intellectual among the
wretched assortment of his workers. Yes, he himself is getting sick
of the diverse social cases, the invalids, the cripples, the cranks. A
fire breaks out, and these fellows will do nothing till the fire
brigade arrives but stand and stare panic-stricken at the flames.
Whenever he is forced to send out one such unstable character he
stays awake for nights thinking what if in an obscure rage, against
society or whatever, the fire watcher should himself set the forest
on fire. He feels certain that he, the man in front of him here,
though occupied with affairs of the mind, will be sufficiently alive
to his duty to abandon his books and fight the fire. Yes, it is a
question of moral values.

Sorry, the old man has forgotten what it is his candidate
wishes to write? A doctorate?

Once more he apologized. He is still, sad to say, at the elementary stages of his study. Yes, he has wasted much time. Indeed,
he has no family.

A young secretary is called in.

Then he is invited to sign an inoffensive little contract for six
months: spring, summer (ah, summer is dangerous!), and half the
autumn. Discipline, responsibility, vigilance, conditions of dis-
missal. A hush descends while he runs his eyes cursorily over the
document. Manager and secretary are ready with a pen, but he
prefers to sign with his own. He signs several copies. First salary
due on the 5th of April. Now he eases himself into his chair,

unable to rise, tired still. He is not used to waking so early. Meanwhile he tries to establish some sort of contact, display an interest. He inquires about the size of the forests, the height of the trees. To tell the truth—he runs on expansively, in a sort of dangerous drowsiness—the fact is that he has never seen a real forest in this country yet. An occasional ancient grove, yes, but he hardly believes (ha-ha-ha) that the authorities in charge of afforestation have anything to do with that. Yes, he keeps hearing over the radio about forests being planted to honor this, that, and the other personage. Though apparently one cannot actually see them yet . . . The trees grow slowly . . . don't gain height . . . Actually he understands . . . this arid soil . . . In other countries, now . . .

At last he falters. Naturally he realizes, has realized from the start, that he has made a bad blunder, has sensed it from the laughter trembling in the girl's eyes, from the shocked fury coloring the face of the manager who is edging his way to old age. The candidate has, to use a tangible image, taken a careless step and trampled a tender spot in the heart of the man in charge of forests, who is fixing him now with a harsh stare and delivering a monologue for his benefit.

What does he mean by small trees? He has obviously failed to use his eyes. Of course there are forests. Real forests. Jungles, no, but forests, yes, indeed. If he will pardon the question: What does he know about what happens in this country anyway? For even when he travels through it on a bus he won't bother to take his head out of his book. It's laughable, really, these flat allegations. He, the old man, has come across this kind of talk from young people, but the candidate is rather past that age. If he, the manager, had the time to spare, he could show him maps. But soon he will see for himself. There are forests in the Hills of Judaea, in Galilee, Samaria, and elsewhere. Perhaps he needs a stronger pair of spectacles. The manager would like to ask the candidate to take spare spectacles with him. He would rather not have any more trouble. Goodbye.

Where are they sending him?

A few days later he is back. This time he is received not by the manager, but by an underling. He is being sent to one of the larger forests. He won't be alone there but with a laborer, an Arab. They feel certain he has no prejudices. Goodbye. Ah yes, departure is on Sunday.

Things happen fast. He severs connections and they appear to come loose with surprising ease. He vacates his room and his landlady is glad of it, for some reason. He spends the last nights with one of his learned friends, who sets to work at once to prepare a study schedule for him. While his zealous friend is busy in one room cramming books into a suitcase, the prospective fire watcher fondles the beloved wife in another. He is pensive, his hands gentle, there is something of joy in his expectations of the morrow. What shall he study? His friends suggest the Crusades. Yes, that would be just right for him. Everyone specializes in a certain subject. He may yet prove to be a little researcher all in his own right just so long as he doesn't fritter his time away. He ought to bring some startling scientific theory back from the forests. His friends will take care of the facts later.

But in the morning, when the lorry of the Afforestation Department comes to fetch him out of his shattered sleep, he suddenly imagines that all this has been set in motion just to get rid of him; and, shivering in the cold morning air, he can but console himself with the thought that this adventure will go the way of all others and be drowned in somnolence. Is it any wonder that Jerusalem, high on its hills, Jerusalem, which is left behind now, is fading like a dream? He abandons himself to the jolts and pitches of the lorry. The laborers with their hoes and baskets sit huddled away from him in the back of the car. They sense that he belongs to another world. The bald patch and the glasses are an indication, one of many.

Traveling half a day.

The lorry leaves the main road and travels over long, alien dirt roads, among nameless new-immigrant settlements. Laborers alight, others take their place. Everyone receives instructions from the driver, who is the one in command around here. We are going south, are we? Wide country meeting a spring-blue sky. The ground is damp still and clods of earth drop off the lorry's tires. It is late in the morning when he discovers the first trees scattered among rocks. Young slender pines, tiny, light green. "Then I was right," he tells himself with a smile. But further on the trees grow taller. Now the light bursts and splinters. Long shadows steal aboard the lorry like stowaways. People keep changing and only the driver, the passenger, and his suitcases stay put. The forests grow denser, no more bare patches now. Pines, always, and only the one species, obstinately, unvaryingly. He is tired, dusty, hungry, has long ago lost all sense of direction. The sun is playing tricks, twisting around him. He does not see where he is going, only what he is leaving behind. At three o'clock the lorry is emptied of laborers and only he is left. For a long time the lorry climbs over a rugged track. He is cross, his mouth feels dry. In despair he tries to pull a book out of one suitcase, but then the lorry stops. The driver gets off, bangs the door, comes around to him and says: "This is it. Your predecessor's already made off—yesterday. Your instructions are all up there. You at least can read, which makes a change."

Laboriously he hauls himself and his two suitcases down. An odd, charming stone house stands on a hill. Pines of all sizes surround it. He is at a high altitude here, though he cannot yet see everything from where he is. Silence, a silence of trees. The driver stretches his legs, looks around breathes the air, then suddenly he nods goodbye and climbs back into his cab and switches the engine on.

He who must stay behind is seized with regret. Despair. What now? Just a minute! He doesn't understand. He rushes at the car, beats his fists against the door, whispers furiously at the surprised driver.

"But food . . . what about food?"

It appears that the Arab takes care of everything.

Alone he trudges uphill, a suitcase in each hand. Gradually the world comes into view. The front door stands open and he enters a large room, the ground floor. Semi-darkness, dilapidated objects on the floor, food remnants, traces of a child. The despair mounts in him. He puts down the suitcases and climbs absent-mindedly to the second floor. The view strikes him with awe. Five hills covered with a dense green growth—pine. A silvery blue horizon with a distant sea. He is instantly excited, forgetting everything. He is even prepared to change his opinion of the Afforestation Department.

A telephone, binoculars, a sheet covered with instructions. A large desk and an armchair beside it. He settles himself into the chair and reads the instructions five times over, from beginning to end. Then he pulls out his pen and makes a few stylistic corrections. He glances fondly at the black instrument. He is in high spirits. He considers calling up one of his friends in town, say something tender to one of his ageing lady-loves. He might announce his safe arrival, describe the view perhaps. Never has he had a public telephone at his disposal yet. He lifts the receiver to his ear. An endless purring. He is not familiar with the proceedings. He tries dialing. In vain. The purr remains steady. At last he dials zero, like a sober citizen expecting a sober reply.

The telephone breaks its silence.

The Fire Brigade comes on with a startled "What's happened?" Real alarm at the other end. (Where? where? confound it!) Before he has said a word, questions rain down on him. How large is the fire? What direction the wind? They are coming at once. He tries to put in a word, stutters, and already they are starting a car over there. Panic grips him. He jumps up, the receiver tight in his hand. He breaks out in a cold sweat. With the last remnant of words in his power he explains everything. No, there is no fire. There is nothing. Only getting acquainted. He has just arrived and wanted to get through to town. His name is so-and-so. That is all.

A hush at the other side. The voice changes. This must be their chief now. Pleased to meet your, sir, we've taken down your name. Have you read all the instructions? Personal calls are quite out of the question. Anyway, you've only just arrived, haven't you? Or is there some urgent need? Your wife? Your children?

No, he has no family.

Well, then, why the panic? Lonely? He'll get used to it. Please don't disturb us unnecessarily in the future. Goodbye.

The ring closes in on him a little. Pink streaks on the horizon. He is tired, hungry. He has risen early, and he is utterly unused to that. This high commanding view makes him dizzy. Needless to add—the silence. He picks up the binoculars with a limp hand and raises them to his eyes. The world leaps close, blurred. Pines lunge at him upright. He adjusts the forest, the hills, the sea on the horizon to the quality of his eyes. He amuses himself a bit, then lets go of the binoculars and eases himself into the chair. He has a clear conception of his new job now. Just watching. His eyes grow heavy. He dozes, sleeps perhaps.

Suddenly he wakes—a red light is burning on his glasses. He is bewildered, scared, his senses heavy. The forest has caught fire, apparently and he has missed it. He jumps up, his heart wildly beating grabs the telephone, the binoculars, and then it occurs to him that it is the sun, only the sun setting beyond the trees. He is facing west. Now he knows. Slowly he drops back into the chair. His heart contracts with something like terror, like emptiness. He imagined himself deserted in this place, forgotten. His glasses mist over and he takes them off and wipes them.

When dusk falls he hears steps.

An Arab and a little girl are approaching the house. Swiftly he rises to his feet. They notice him, look up and stop in their tracks—startled by the soft, scholarly-looking figure. He bows his head. They walk but their steps are hesitant now. He goes down to them.

The Arab turns out to be old and mute. His tongue was cut out during the war. By one of them or one of us? Does it matter? Who knows what the last words were that stuck in his throat? In the dark room, its windows ablaze with the last light, the fire watcher shakes a heavy hand, bends to pat the child, who flinches, terrified. The ring of loneliness closes in on him. The Arab puts on lights. The fire watcher will sleep upstairs.

The first evening, and a gnawing sadness. The weak yellow light of the bulbs is depressing. For the time being he draws comfort only from the wide view, from the soft blue of the sea in the distance and the sun surrendering to it. He sits cramped on his chair and watches the big forests entrusted to his eyes. He imagines that the fire may break out at any moment. After a long delay the Arab brings up his supper. An odd taste, a mixture of tastes. But he devours everything, leaves not a morsel. His eyes rove hungrily between the plate and the thick woods. Suddenly, while chewing, he discovers a few faraway lights—villages. He broods awhile about women, then takes off his clothes, opens the suitcase that does not hold books and takes out his things. It seems a long time since he left town. He wraps himself in blankets, lies facing the forests. A cool breeze caresses him. What sort of sleep will come to one here? The Arab brings him a cup of coffee to help him stay awake. The fire watcher would like to talk to him about something; perhaps about the view, or about the poor lighting perhaps. He has words left in him still from the city. But the Arab does not understand Hebrew. The fire watcher smiles wearily in thanks. Something about his bald crown, the glint of his glasses, seems to daunt the Arab.

It is half-past nine—the beginning of the night. Cicadas strike up. He struggles against sleep engulfing him. His eyes close and his conscience tortures him. The binoculars dangle from their strap around his neck, and from time to time he picks them up, lifts them to his eyes blinded with sleep, glass clicking against glass. He opens his eyes in a stare and finds himself in the forest, among pines, hunting for flames. Darkness.

How long does it take for a forest to burn down? Perhaps he will only look every hour, every two hours. Even if the forest should start to burn he would still manage to raise the alarm in time to save the rest. The murmur downstairs has died down. The Arab and his child are asleep. And he is up here, lightheaded, tired after his journey, between three walls and a void gaping to the sea. He must not roll over onto his other side. He nods, and his sleep is pervaded by the fear of fire, fire stealing upon him unawares. At midnight he transfers himself from bed to chair; it is safer that way. His head droops heavily onto the desk, his spine aches, he is crying out for sleep, full of regret, alone against the dark empire swaying before him. Till at last the black hours of the first night pass; till out of the corner of his eye he sees the morning grow among the hills.

Only fatigue makes him stay on after the first night. The days and nights following revolve as on a screen, a misty, dreamlike screen lit up once every twenty-four hours by the radiant glow of the setting sun. It is not himself but a stranger who wanders those first days between the two stories of the house, the binoculars slung across his chest, absently chewing on the food left him by the unseen Arab. The heavy responsibility that has suddenly fallen upon his shoulders bewilders him. Hardest of all is the silence. Even with himself he hardly manages to exchange a word. Will he be able to open a book here? The view amazes and enchants him still and he cannot have enough of it. After ten days of anguish he is himself again. In one brief glance he can embrace all the five hills now. He has learned to sleep with his eyes open. Lo, a new accomplishment; rather interesting, one must admit.

At last the other suitcase, the one with the books, gets opened, with a slight delay of but a fortnight or so. The delay does not worry him in the least, for aren't the spring, the summer, and half the autumn still before him? The first day is devoted to sorting the books, spelling out titles, thumbing the pages. One can't deny that there is some pleasure in handling the fat, fragrant, annotated volumes. The texts are in English, the quotations all in Latin. Strange phrases from alien worlds. He worries a little. His subject—"The Crusades." From the human, that is to say, the ecclesiastical aspect. He has not gone into particulars yet. "Crusades," he whispers softly to himself and feels joy rising in him at the word the sound. He feels certain that there is some dark issue buried within the subject and that it will startle him, startle others in him. And it will be just out of this drowsiness that envelops his mind like a permanent cloud that the matter will be revealed to him.

The following day is spent on pictures. The books are rich in illustrations. Odd funny ones. Monks, cardinals; a few blurred kings, thin knights, tiny, villainous Jews. Curious landscapes, maps. He studies them, compares, dozes. On the hard road to the abstract he wishes to linger awhile with the concrete. That night he is kept off his studies by a gnat. Next morning he tells himself: "Oh wondrous time, how fast it flies upon these lonely summits." He opens the first book on the first page, reads the author's preface, his grateful acknowledgments. He reads other prefaces, various acknowledgments, publication data. He checks a few dates. At noon his mind is distracted from the books by an imaginary flame flashing among the trees. He remains tense for hours, excited, searching with the binoculars, his hand on the telephone. At last, towards evening, he discovers that it is only the red dress of the Arab's little daughter who is skipping among the trees. The following day, when he is all set to decipher the first page, his father turns up suddenly with a suitcase in his hand.

"What's happened?" the father asks anxiously.

"Nothing . . . Nothing's happened . . . "

"But what made you become a forester then?"

"A bit of solitude . . . "

"Solitude . . . " he marvels. "You want solitude?"

The father bends over the open book, removes his heavy glasses, and peers closely at the text. "The Crusades," he murmurs. "Is that what you're engaged on?"

"Yes."

"Aren't I disturbing you in your work? I haven't come to disturb you . . . I have a few days' leave."

"No, you're not disturbing me."

"Magnificent view."

"Yes, magnificent."

"You're thinner."

"Could be."

"Couldn't you study in the libraries?"

Apparently not. Silence. The father sniffs around the room like a little hedgehog. At noon he asks his son:

"Do you think it is lonely here? That you'll find solitude?"

"Yes, what's to disturb me?"

"I'm not going to disturb you."

"Of course not. What makes you think that!"

"I'll go away soon."

"No, don't go. Please stay."

The father stays a week.

In the evening the father tries to become friendly with the Arab and his child. A few words of Arabic have stuck in his memory from the days of his youth, and he will seize any occasion to fill them with meaning. But his pronunciation is unintelligible to the Arab, who only nods his head dully.

They sit together, not speaking. The son cannot read a single line with the father there, even though the father keeps muttering: "Don't bother about me. I'll keep myself in the background." At night the father sleeps on the bed and the fire watcher stretches himself out on the floor. Sometimes the father wakes in the night to find his son awake. "Perhaps we could take turns," he says. "You go to sleep on the bed and I'll watch the forest." But the son knows that his father will see not a forest but a blurred stain. He won't notice the fire till it singes his clothes. In the daytime they change places—the son lies on the bed and the father sits by the desk and tries to read the book, which lies open still. How he would like to strike up a conversation with his son, stir up some discussion. For example, he fails to understand why his son won't deal with the Jews, the Jewish aspect of the Crusades. For isn't mass suicide a wonderful and terrible thing? The son gives him a kindly grin, a noncommittal reply, and silence. During the last days of his visit the father occupies himself with the dumb Arab. A host of questions bubbles up in him. Who is the man? Where is he from? Who cut his tongue out? Why? Look, he has seen hatred in the man's eyes. A creature like that may yet set the forest on fire someday. Why not?

On his last day the father is given the binoculars to play with.

Suitcase in hand, back bent, he shakes his son's hand. Then— tears in the eyes of the little father.

"I've been disturbing you, I know I have . . . "

In vain does the son protest, mumble about the oceans of time still before him—about half the spring, the whole long summer, half the distant autumn.

From his elevated seat he watches his lost blind father fumbling for the back of the lorry. The driver is rude and impatient with him. When the lorry moves off the father waves goodbye to the forest by mistake. He has lost his bearings.

For a week he crawls from line to line over the difficult text. After every sentence he raises his head to look at the forest. He is still awaiting a fire. The air grows hot. A haze shimmers above the sea on the horizon. When the Arab returns at dusk his garments are damp with sweat, the child's gestures are tired. Anyway you look at it, he himself is lucky. At such a time to be here, high above any town. Ostensibly, he is working all the time, but observing could hardly be called work, could it? The temperature rises day by day. He wonders whether it is still spring, of whether perhaps the summer has already crept upon the world. One can gather nothing from the forest, which shows no change, except thorns fading to yellow among the trees perhaps. His hearing has grown acute. The sound of trees whispers incessantly in his ears. His eyes shine with the sun's gaining strength, his senses grown keen. He is becoming attached to the forest in a way. Even his dreams are growing richer in trees. The women sprout leaves.

His text is difficult, the words distant. It has turned out to be only the preface to a preface. But, being as diligent as he is, he does not skip a single passage. He translates every word, then rewrites the translation in rhyme. Simple, easy rhymes, in order that the words should merge in his mind, should not escape into the silence.

No wonder that by Friday he can count but three pages read, out of the thousands. "Played out," he whispers to himself and trails his fingertips over the desk. Perhaps he'll take a rest? A pensive air comes over the green empire before him each Sabbath eve and makes his heart contract. Though he believes neither in God nor in all his angels, there is a sacredness that brings a lump to his throat.

He combs his beard in honor of the holy day. Yes, there is a new beard growing here along with the pines. He brings some order into the chaos of his room, picks a page off the floor. What is this? The instruction sheet. Full of interest he reads it once more and discovers a forgotten instruction, or one added by his own hand, perhaps.

"Let the forest scout go out from time to time for a short walk among the trees, in order to sharpen his senses."

His first steps in the forest proper are like a baby's. He circles the observation post, hugging its walls as though afraid to leave them. Yet the trees attract him like magic. Little by little he ventures among the hills, deeper and deeper. If he should smell burning he will run back.

But this isn't a forest yet, only the hope and promise of one. Here and there the sun appears through the foliage and a traveler among the trees is dappled with flickers of light. This isn't a rustling forest but a very small one, like a graveyard. A forest of solitudes. The pines stand erect, slim, serious; like a company of new recruits awaiting their commander. The roaming fire watcher is pleased by the play of light and shadow. With every step he crushes dry pine needles underfoot. Softly, endlessly the pines shed their needles; pines arrayed in a garment of mingling life and death.

The rounded human moving among trees whose yearning is so straight, so fierce. His body aches a bit, the ache of cramped limbs stretching; his legs are heavy. Suddenly he catches sight of the telephone line. A yellowish wire smelling of mould. Well, so this is his contact with the world. He starts tracing the yellow wire, searching for its origin, is charmed by its pointless twists and loops between the trees. They must have let some joker unwind the drum over the hills.

Suddenly he hears voices. He wavers, stops, then sees the little clearing in the wood. The Arab is seated on a pile of rocks, his hoe by his side. The child is talking to him excitedly, describing something with animated gestures. The scout tiptoes nearer, as lightly as his bulk will permit. They are instantly aware of him, sniff his alien being, and fall silent. The Arab jumps up, stands by his hoe as though hiding something. He faces them, wordless. It is the Sabbath eve today, isn't it, and there is a yearning in his heart. He stands and stares, for all the world like a supervisor bothered by some obscure triviality. The soft breeze caresses his eyes. If he did not fear for his standing with them he would hum them a little tune, perhaps. He smiles absently, his eyes stray, and slowly he withdraws; with as much dignity as he can muster.

The two remain behind, petrified. The child's voice has shriveled halfway through her interrupted story, the Arab starts weeding the thorns at his feet. But the scout has retreated already, gone forth into the empire. He has been wandering in the woods for all of an hour now and is still making new discoveries. The names of donors, for example. It had never occurred to him that this wouldn't be just some anonymous forest but one with a name, and not just one name either. Many rocks bear copper plates, brilliantly brushed. He stoops, takes off his glasses, reads: Louis Schwartz of Chicago, the King of Burundi and his People. Flickers of light play over the letters. The names cling to him, like the falling pine needles that slip into his pocket. How odd! The tired memory tries to refresh itself with these faceless names. Name after name is absorbed by him as he walks, and by the time he reaches the observation post he can already hold a little rehearsal. He recites the assorted names, a vacuous smile on his face.

Friday night.

A wave of sadness wells within him. His mind happens to be perfectly lucid at the moment. "We'll clear out on Sunday," he whispers suddenly, and starts humming a snatch of song; inaudibly at first, the sound humming inside him, but soon trilling and rising high to the darkening sky. A hidden abyss behind him echoes in reply. The light drips, drips. Strings of light tear the sunset across and he shouts song at it, shrills recklessly, wanton with solitude. He starts one song, stops, plunges into another without change of key. His eyes fill with tears. The dark stifles his throat at last, he hears himself suddenly and falls silent.

Peace returns to the forest. Relics of light linger. Five minutes pass and then the Arab and the girl emerge from the cover of the underbrush and hurry to the house with bent heads.

The Sabbath passes in a wonderful tranquillity. He is utterly calm. He has begun counting the trees for a change. On Sunday he is on the verge of escaping but then the lorry brings him his salary, a part of the job he had forgotten. He is amazed, gushes his thanks to the mocking driver. So there's a prize in the whispering world, is there? He returns to the books.

Hot summer. Yes, but we have forgotten the birds. Presumably the observation post stands on an ancient crossroads of bird trajectories. How else to explain the mad flocks swooping in from the forest to beat their wings against the walls, drop on the bed, dive at the books, shed gray feathers and green dung, shatter the dull air with their restlessness—and vanish on their circuitous flight to the sea. A change has come over him. Sunburned, yes, but there is more to it than that. The heat wells up in him, frightens him. A dry flow of desert wind may rouse the forest to suicide; hence he redoubles his vigilance, presses the binoculars hard against his eyes, and subjects the forest in his charge to a strict survey. How far has he come? Some slight twenty pages are behind him, thousands still before. What does he remember? A few words, the tail end of a theory, the atmosphere on the eve of the Crusades. The nights are peaceful. He could have studied, could have concentrated, were it not for the gnats. Night after night he extinguishes the lights and sits in darkness. The words have dropped away from him like husks. Cicadas. Choruses of jackals. A bat wings heavily across the gloom. Rustlings.

Hikers start arriving in the forest. Lone hikers some of them, but mostly they come in groups. He follows them through the binoculars. Various interesting ages. Like ants they swarm over the forest, pour in among the trees, calling out to each other, laughing; then they cast off their rucksacks all at once, unburden themselves of as many clothes as possible and hang them up on branches, and promptly come over to the house.

Water is what they want. Water!

He comes down to them, striking them with wonder. The bald head among the green pines, the heavy glasses. Indeed, everything indicates an original character.

He stands by the water tap, firm and upright, and slakes their thirst. Everyone begs permission to go upstairs for a look at the view. He consents, joyfully. They crowd into his little room and utter the stock formulae of admiring exclamations. He smiles as though he had created it all. Above everything, they are surprised by the sea. They had never imagined one could see the sea from here. Yet how soon they grow bored! One glance, a cry of admiration, and they grow restless and eager to be away. They peep at his notes, at the heavy books, and descend the staircase brimming with veneration for him and his view. The group leaders ask him to give some account of the place, but there is no account to give. Everything is still artificial here. There is nothing here, not even some archeology for amateurs, nothing but a few donors' names, inscribed on rocks. Would they be interested in the names? Well, for instance . . .

They laugh.

The girls look at him kindly. No, he isn't handsome. But might he not become engraved on one of their hearts?

They light campfires.

They wish to cook their food, or to warm themselves. A virtuous alarm strikes him. Tiny flames leap up in the forest, a bluish smoke starts blowing gaily about the treetops. A fire? Yes and no. He stays glued, through his binoculars, to the lively figures.

Towards evening he goes to explore his flickering, merrymaking empire. He wishes to sound a warning. Softly, soundlessly he draws near the campfire, the figures wreathed in flames. He approaches them unnoticed, and they are startled when they discover him beside them. Dozens of young eyes look up at him together. The leaders rise at once.

"Yes? What do you want?"

"The fire. Be careful! One spark, and the forest may burn down."

They are quick to assure him. Laying their hands on their young hearts they give him their solemn promise to watch, with all their eyes shining in a row before him. They will keep within bounds, of course they will, what does he think?

He draws aside. Appeased? Yes and no. There, among the shadows, in the twilight of the fire, he lingers and lets his eyes rove. The girls and their bare creamy legs, slender does. The flames crackle and sing, softly, gently. He clenches his fists in pain. If only he could warm his hands a little.

"Like to join us?" they ask politely. His vertical presence is faintly embarrassing.

No, thanks. He can't. He is busy. His studies. They have seen the books, haven't they? Now there is nothing for it but to withdraw with measured tread. But as soon as he has vanished from their view he flings himself behind the trees, hides among the needle branches. He looks at the fire from afar, at the girls, till everything fades and blankets are spread for sleep. Giggles, girls'

affected shrieks, leaders' rebukes. Before he can begin to think,
select one out of the many figures, it will be dawn. Silence is still
best. At midnight he feels his way through the trees, back to the
observation post. He sits in his place, waiting. One of the figures
may be working its way in the darkness towards him. But no, nothing. They are tired, already sleeping.

And the same the next day, and all the days following.

Early in the morning he opens his book and hears wild
singing in the distance. He does not raise his eyes from the page
but his hand strays to the binoculars. A dappled silence. Flashes of
light through branches. His eyes are faithful to the written page,
but his thoughts have gone whoring already. From the corner of
his eye he follows the procession threading through the forest—
sorting, checking ages, colors, joys of youth. There is something of
abandonment about them from afar, like a procession of Crusaders; except that these women are bare. He trembles, choking
suddenly. He removes his glasses and beats his head against the
books. Half an hour later they arrive. Asking for water to drink
and the view to look at, as usual. They have heard about the wonderful view to be seen from up here. Perhaps they have heard
about the scholar as well, but they say nothing. The group leaders
take them, a batch at a time, into his room turned public property. No sooner have they scattered about the forest than the
campfires leap up, as though that were their prime necessity. In
the evening he rushes over the five hills, from fire to fire, impelled by his duty to warn them or by an obscure desire to reveal
himself. He never joins any of the circles though. He prefers to
hide in the thicket. Their singing throbs in his heart, and even
more than that—the whisperings. Warm summer nights—something constantly seeping through the leaves.

Gradually the groups of hikers blend. One excursion leaves,
another arrives. By the time he has managed to learn a few outstanding names their owners are gone and the sounds alone survive among the branches. Languor comes over him. No longer
does he trouble to caution against fire. On the contrary. He would
welcome a little conflagration, a little local tumult. The hikers,
however, are extremely responsible. They themselves take care to
stamp out every dying ember. Their leaders come in advance to
set his mind at rest.

The birds know how much he as neglected his studies; the
birds whom he watches constantly lest they approach his desk. A
month has passed since he last turned a page and he is stuck
squirming between two words. He says: let the heat abate, the

hikers be gone—then I shall race over the lines. If only he could skip the words and get to the essence. From time to time he scribbles in his notebook. Stray thoughts, speculations, musings, outlines of assumptions. Not much. A sentence a day. He would like to gain a hold upon it all indirectly. Yet he is doubtful whether he has gained a hold even upon the forest in front of his eyes. Look, here the Arab and the girl are disappearing among the trees and he cannot find them. Towards evening they emerge from an unforeseen direction as though the forest had conceived them even now. They tread the soil softly. They avoid people, choose roundabout ways. He smiles at them both but they recoil.

Friday. The forest is overrun, choking with people. They come on foot and by car, crowds disgorged by the faraway cities. Where is his solitude now? He sprawls on his chair like a dethroned king whose empire has slipped from his hands. Twilight lingers on the treetops. Sabbath eve. His ears alone can catch, beyond the uproar of voices, beyond the rustling, the thin cry of the weary soil ceaselessly crushed by the teeth of young roots. A hikers' delegation comes to see him. They just want to ask him a question. They have argued, laid wagers, and he shall be their arbiter. Where exactly is this Arab village that is marked on the map? It ought to be somewhere around here, an abandoned Arab village. Here, they even know its name, something like . . . Actually, it must be right here, right in the forest . . . Does he know anything about it perhaps? They're simply curious.

The fire watcher gives them a tired look. "A village?" he repeats with a polite, indulgent smile at their folly. No, there is no village here. The map must be wrong, the surveyor's hand must have shaken.

But in the small hours of the night, somewhere between a doze and a slumber, in the face of the whispering, burgeoning forest, the name floats back into his mind all of a sudden and he is seized with restlessness. He descends to the ground floor, feels his way in the dark to the bed of the Arab, who lies asleep covered with rags. Roughly he wakes him and whispers the name of the village. The Arab does not understand. His eyes are consumed with weariness. The fire watcher's accent must be at fault. He tries again, therefore, repeats the name over and over and the Arab listens and suddenly he understands. An expression of surprise, of wonder and eagerness suffuses all his wrinkles. He jumps up, stands there in his hairy nakedness, and flings up a heavy arm in the direction of the window, pointing fervently, hopelessly, at the forest.

The fire watcher thanks him and departs, leaving the big naked figure in the middle of the room. When he wakes tomorrow, the Arab will think he has dreamed it.

Ceremonies. A season of ceremonies. The forest turns ceremonial. The trees stand bowed, heavy with honor, they take on meaning, they belong. White ribbons are strung to delimit new domains. Luxurious coaches struggle over the rocky roads, a procession of shining automobiles before and behind. Sometimes they are preceded by a motorcycle mounted by an excited policeman. Unwieldy around them. Little by little they assemble, crush out cigarettes with their black shoes, and fall silent—paying homage to the memory of themselves. The fire watcher, too, participates in the ceremony, from afar, he and his binoculars. A storm of obedient applause breaks out, a gleam of scissors, a flash of photographers, ribbons sag. A plaque is unveiled, a new little truth is revealed to the world. A brief tour of the conquered wood, and then the distinguished gathering dissolves into its various vehicles and sallies forth.

Where is the light gone?

In the evening, when the fire watcher comes down to the drooping ribbons, to the grateful trees, he will find nothing but a pale inscription saying, for example: "Donated by the Sackson children in honor of Daddy Sackson of Baltimore, a fond tribute to his paternity. End of Summer Nineteen Hundred and . . . "

Sometimes the fire watcher, observing from his heights, will notice one of the party darting troubled looks about him, raising his eyes at the trees as though searching for something. It takes many ceremonies before the fire watcher's wandering mind will grasp that this is none other than the old man in charge of afforestation, who comes and repeats himself, dressed always in the same clothes, at every ceremony.

Once he goes down to him. The old man is walking among his distinguished foreign party, is jesting with them haltingly in their language. The fire watcher comes out of the trees and plants himself in front of him for the inevitable encounter. The distinguished party stops, startled. An uneasy silence falls over them. The ladies shrink back.

"What do you want?" demands the old man masterfully.

The fire watcher gives a weak smile.

"Don't you know me? I'm the watchman. That is to say, the fire watcher . . . employee of yours . . . "

"Ah!" fist beating against aged forehead, "I didn't recognize you, was alarmed, these tatters have changed your appearance so, this heavy beard. Well young man, and how's the solitude?"

"Solitude?" he wonders.

The old man presents him to the party.

"A scholar . . . "

They smile, troubled, meet his hand with their fingertips, move on. They do not have complete faith in his cleanliness. The old man on the other hand, looks at him affectionately. A thought crosses his mind and he stays a moment.

"Well, so there *are* forests," he grins with good-natured irony.

"Yes," admits the scout honestly. "Forests, yes . . . but . . . "

"But what?"

"But fires, no."

"Fires?" the old man wonders, bending towards him.

"Yes, fires. I spend whole days here sitting and wondering. Such a quiet summer."

"Well, why not? Actually, there hasn't been a fire in here for several years now. To tell you the truth, I don't think there has ever been a fire at all in this forest. Nature itself is harnessed to our great enterprise here, ha-ha."

"And I was under the impression . . . "

"That what?"

"That fires broke out here every other day. By way of illustration, at least. The whole machinery waiting on the alert, is it all for nothing? The fire engines . . . telephone lines . . . the manpower . . . for months my eyes have been strained with waiting."

"Waiting? Ha-ha, what a joke!"

The old one hurries along. The drivers are switching on their engines. That is all he needs, to be left overnight in this arboreal silence. Before he goes he would just like to know the watchman's opinion of the dumb Arab. The lorry driver has got the idea into his head that the fellow is laying in a stock of kerosene . . .

The watchman is stirred. "Kerosene?"

"Daresay it's some fancy of that malicious driver. This Arab is a placid kind of fellow, isn't he?"

"Wonderfully placid," agrees the fire watcher eagerly. Then he walks a few steps around the old man and whispers confidentially: "Isn't he a local?"

"A local?"

"Because our forest is growing over, well, over a ruined village . . . "

"A village?"

"A small village."

"A small village? Ah—" (Something is coming back to him anyway.) "Yes, there used to be some sort of a farmstead here. But that is a thing of the past."

Of the past, yes, certainly. What else . . . ?

One day's program as an example.

Not having slept at night, he does not wake up in the morning. Light springs up between his fingers. What date is today? There is no telling. Prisoners score lines on the walls of their cell, but he is not in prison. He has come of his own free will, and so he will go. He could lift the receiver and find out the date from the firemen bent over their fire engines, waiting in some unknown beyond, but he does not want to scare them yet.

He goes down to the tap and sprinkles a few drops of water over his beard to freshen it up. The he climbs back to his room, snatches up the binoculars, and makes a pre-breakfast inspection. Excitement grips him. The forest filled with smoke? No, the binoculars are to blame. He wipes the lenses with a corner of his grimy shirt. The forest clears up at once, disappointingly. None of the trees has done any real growing overnight.

He goes down again. He picks up the dry loaf of bread and cuts himself a rough slice. He chews rapidly, his eyes roving over a torn strip of newspaper in which tomatoes are wrapped. It is not, God forbid, out of a hunger for news but so as to keep his eyes in training lest they forget the shape of the printed letter. He returns to his observation post, his mouth struggling with an enormous half-rotten tomato. He sucks, swallows, gets smeared with the red trickling sap. At last he throws a sizeable remnant away. Silence. He dozes a bit, wakes, looks for a long time at the treetops. The day stretches out ahead of him. Softly he draws near the books.

Where are we? How many pages read? Better not count them or he will fall prey to despair; for the time being he is serene, and why spoil it? It isn't a question of quantity, is it? And he remembers what he has read up to now perfectly well, forwards and backwards. The words wave and whirl within him. For the time being, therefore, for the past few weeks, that is, he has been devoting his zeal to one single sheet of paper. A picture? Rather, a map. A map of the area. He will display it on this wall here for the benefit of his successors, that they may remember him. Look, he has signed his name already, signed it to begin with, lest he forget.

What is he drawing? Trees. But not only trees. Hills too, a blue horizon too. He is improving day by day. If he had colored crayons he could have added some birds as well; at least, say, those native to the area. What interests him in particular is the village buried beneath the trees. That is to say, it hasn't always been as silent here. His curiosity is of a strictly scientific nature. What was it the old man had said? "A scholar." He strokes the beard and his hand lingers, disentangles a few hairs matted with filth. What time is it? Early still. He reads a line about the attitude of the Pope to the German Kaiser and falls asleep. He wakes with a start. He lights a cigarette, tosses the burning match out into the forest, but the match goes out in midair. He flings the cigarette butt among the trees and it drops on a stone and burns itself out in solitude.

He gets up, paces about restlessly. What time is it? Early still.

He goes in search of the Arab, to say good morning. He must impress his own vigilant existence upon the man, lest he be murdered some morning between one doze and another. Ever since the fire watcher has spoken the name of the vanished village in his ears the Arab has become suspicious, as though he were being watched all the time. The fire watcher strides rapidly between the pines. How light his footstep has grown during the long summer months. His soundless appearance startles the two.

"Shalom," he says, in Hebrew.

They reply in two voices. The child—a voice that has sweetness in it, the Arab—a harsh grunt. The fire watcher smiles to himself and hurries on as though he was extremely busy. Chiseled stones lie scattered among the trees, outlines of buildings, ruins, and relics. He searches for marks left by humans. Everyday he comes and disturbs a few stones, looking for traces.

A man and a woman are lying here entwined, like statues toppled from their base. Their terror when the bearded head bends silently over them! Smile at them and run, you! A couple slipped away from a group hike, no doubt.

What is he looking for? Relics of thoughts that have flitted here, words that have completed their mission. But what will he find one fine day, say even the day that we have taken for a sample? Small tins filled with kerosene. How wonderful! The zeal with which someone has filled tin after tin here and covered them up with the girl's old dress. He stoops over the treasure, the still liquid on whose face dead pine needles drift. His reflection floats back at him together with the faint smell.

Blissfully he returns to the house, opens a tin of meat, and bolts its content to the last sliver. He wipes his mouth and spits far out among the branch-filled air. He turns two pages of a book and reads the Cardinal's reply to a Jew's epistle. Funny, these twists and turns of the Latin, but what a threat is conveyed by them. He falls asleep, wakes, realizes he has nearly missed an important ceremony on the easternmost hill. From now on the binoculars stay glued to his eyes and he mingles with the distinguished crowd from afar. He can even make out the movements of the speaker's lips; he will fill in the missing sound himself. But then the flames of the sunset catch his eye and divert his attention, and with a daily returning excitement he becomes absorbed in the splendor, the terrible splendor.

Afterwards he wipes the dust off the silent telephone. To give him his due—he bestows meticulous care on the equipment that belongs to the Afforestation Department, whereas his own equipment is already falling apart. The loose buttons shed among the trees, the frayed shirt, the ragged trousers.

A private outing of joyriders arrives with a loud fanfare to spend the night in the forest. Wearily he chews his supper. Nightfall brings the old familiar sadness.

The Arab and his daughter go to bed. Darkness. The first giggle that emerges from the trees is a slap in his listening face. He turns over a few dark pages, swats a gnat, whistles.

Night. He does not fall asleep.

Then it is the end of summer. The forest is emptying. And with the first autumn wind, who is blown to him like a withered leaf but his ageing mistress, the wife of the friend who sent him here. Clad in summer frock she comes, a wide-brimmed straw hat on her head. Then she clicks her high heels around his room, rummaging through his drawers, bending over the books, peering through the papers. She had gone for a brief vacation by herself somewhere in this neighborhood and had remembered him. How is it when a man sits solitary, facing the forest night after night? She had wanted to surprise him. Well, and what has he come up with? A fresh crusade perhaps? She is awfully curious. Her husband speaks well of him too. In this solitude, among the trees, says the husband, he may yet flower into greatness.

The fire watcher is moved. Without a word he points at the map on the wall. She trips over to look, does not understand. Actually she is interested in texts. What has he written? She is very tired. Such a time till she found this place and she's more dead than alive. The view is pretty, yes, but the place looks awfully neglected. Who lives downstairs? The Arab? Is that so! She met him on the way, tried to ask him something and suddenly—the shock! Dumb, his severed tongue. But the Afforestation Department— hats off to them. Who would have imagined such forests growing in this country! He has changed, though. Grown fatter? This new beard of his is just awful. Why doesn't he say something?

She sinks down on to the bed.

Then he rises, approaches her with that quiet that is in his blood now. He removes her hat, crouches at her feet, unbuckles her shoes; he is trembling with desire, choking.

She is shocked. She draws back her bare tired feet at once with something of terror, perhaps with relief. But he has already let go, stands holding the binoculars and looks at the forest, looks long, peering through the trees, waiting for fire. Slowly he turns to her, the binoculars at his eyes, turns the lenses upon her mischievously, sees the tiny wrinkles whittled in her face, the sweat drops, her fatigue. She smiles at him as in an old photograph. But when the moment drags, her smile turns into protest. She draws herself together crossly, holds up a hand: "Hey, you! Stop it!"

Only towards sunset does he finally manage to undress her. The binoculars are still on his chest, pressed between their bodies. From time to time he coolly interrupts his kisses and caresses, raises the binoculars to his eyes and inspects the forest.

"Duty," he whispers apologetically, sending an odd smile to the nude, ashamed woman. Everything mingles with the glory of the crimson sun—the distant blue of the sea, the still trees, the blood on his cracked lips, the despair, the futility, the loneliness of the act. Accidentally her hand touches that bald crown and flinches.

When the Arab returns it is all over. She is lying in the tangle of her clothes, drowsy. A beautiful night has descended on the world. He sits by his desk, what else should he do? The dark transforms her into a silhouette. The forest bewitches her. Suddenly she rouses herself. The soft voice of the little Arab girl sends a shiver through her. What is she doing here? She dresses rapidly, buttons, buckles. Her voice floats in the darkness.

Actually, she has come out of pity. No one had thought he would persist so long. When does he sleep anyway? She has been sent here to deliver him, deliver him from this solitude. His silence arouses suspicions. Her husband and his friends have suddenly begun to wonder, have become afraid, ha-ha, afraid that he may outshine them all with some brilliant research.

A sudden dark breeze bursts into the room through the gap where there is no wall, whirls around for a little, and dies out in the two corners. He is kindled. His eyes glow.

"Pity? No, unnecessary. When do I sleep? Always . . . though different from the city sleep. Leave here now, just like that? Too late. I haven't finished counting the trees yet. Novel ideas? Maybe, though not what they imagine . . . not exactly scientific . . . Rather, human . . . "

Does she wish him to accompany her on her way back through the forest, or would she go by herself perhaps?

She jumps up.

They cut diagonally across the hills. He walks in front, she drags behind, staggering over the rocks in her high heels, hurt and humiliated. Though thickset, his feet are light and he slips through the foliage swift as a snake, never turning his head. She struggles with the branches whipping back behind him. The moonlight reveals them on their silent trip. What do you say now, my autumn love? Have I gone completely out of my mind? But that was to be expected, wasn't it? Out of my round of pleasures you have cast me into solitude. Trees have taken the place of words for men, forests the place of books. That is all. Eternal autumn, needles falling endlessly on my eyes. I am still awaiting a conflagration.

Wordless, they reach the black main road. Her heels click on the asphalt with a last fury. Now he looks at her. Her face is scratched, her arms bloodstained. How assertively the forest leaves its mark. She contains the thin cry rising in her. Her silence grants her dignity. After some minutes a sleek car driven by a lone gray-templed man halts at her waving hand. She joins him in the car without a parting word. She will yet crumble between his fingers on the long road.

He turns in his tracks. After a few paces the Arab pops up in front of him. He is breathing heavily, his face is dull. And what do you have to say, mister? From where have you sprung now? The Arab holds out her forgotten hat, the straw hat. The fire watcher smiles his thanks, spreads his arms in a gesture of nothing we can do, she's gone. But how amazing, this attention. Nothing will escape the man's eye. He takes the hat from the Arab and pitches it on top of his own head, gives him a slight bow, and the other is immediately alarmed. His face is alert, watching. Together, in silence, they return to the forest, their empire, theirs alone. The fire watcher strides ahead and the Arab tramples on his footsteps. A few clouds, a light breeze. Moonlight pours over the branches and makes them transparent. He leads the Arab over roads that are the same roads always. Barefoot he walks, the Arab, and so still. Round and round he is led, roundabout and to his hideout, amid chiseled stones and silence. The Arab's steps falter. His footfalls lag, die, and come alive again. A deathly cold grips the fire watcher's heart, his hands freeze. He kneels on the rustling earth. Who will give him back all the empty hours? The forest is dark and empty. No one there. Not one campfire. Just now, when he would like to dip his hands in fire, warm them a little. He heaps up some brown needles, takes a match, lights it, and the match goes out at once. He takes another and cups his hands around it, strikes, and this one too flares up and dies. The air is damp and traitorous. He rises. The Arab watches him, a gleam of lunatic hope in his eyes. Softly the fire watcher walks around the pile of stones to the sorry little hideout, picks up a tin of clear liquid and empties it over the heap of pine needles, tosses in a burning match and leaps up with the surging flame—singed, happy. At last he, too, is lit up a little. Stunned, the Arab goes down on his knees. The fire watcher spreads his palms over the flame and the Arab does likewise. Their bodies press in on the fire, which has already reached its highest pitch. He might leave the flame now and go and bathe in the sea. Time, time wasting here among the trees, will do his work for him. He muses, his mind distracted. The fire shows signs of languishing, little by little it dies at his feet. The Arab's face takes on a look of bitter disappointment. Thus far it was only a lesson. The wandering mind of the fire watcher trembles between compromises. He rises wearily and leaves. The Arab slouches in his wake.

Who is sitting on the chair behind the book-laden desk? The child. Her eyes are wide open, drinking in the dark. The Arab has put her there to replace the loving fire watcher. It's an idea.

Strange days follow. We would say: autumn; but that means nothing yet. The needles seem to fall faster, the sun grows weaker, clouds come to stay and a new wind. His mind is slipping, growing unhinged. The ceremonies are over. The donors have gone back to their countries, the hikers to their work, pupils to their study. His own books lie jumbled in a glow of dust. He is neglecting his duties, has left his chair, his desk, his faithful binoculars, and has begun roving endlessly about the forest, by day and by night; a broken twig in his hand, he slashes at the young tree trunks as he walks, as though marking them. Suddenly he slumps down, rests his head against a shining copper plaque, removes his glasses and peers through the blurring foliage, searches the gray sky. Something like a wail, suddenly. Foul fantasies. Then he collects himself once more, jumps up to wander through the wood, among the thistles and rocks. The idea has taken hold in his dim consciousness that he is being called insistently to an encounter at the edge of the forest, at its other end. But when he plunges out of the forest and arrives there, whether it be at night or at noon or in the early dawn, he finds nothing but a yellow waste, a strange wadi, a kind of cursed dream. And he will stand there for a long time, facing the empty treeless silence and feeling that the encounter is taking place, is being successful even though it happens wordlessly. He has spent a whole spring and a long summer never once properly sleeping, and what wonder is it if these last days should be like a trance.

He has lost all hope of fire. Fire has no hold over this forest. He can therefore afford to stay among the trees, not facing them. In order to soothe his conscience he sits the girl in his chair. It has taken less than a minute to teach her the Hebrew word for "fire." How she has grown up during his stay here! She is like a noble mare now with marvelous eyes. Unexpectedly her limbs have ripened, her filth become a woman's smell. At first her old father had been forced to chain her to the chair, or she would have escaped. Yes, the old Arab has grown very attached to the negligent fire watcher, follows him wherever he goes.

Ever since the night when the two of them hugged the little bonfire the Arab, too, has grown languid. He has abandoned his eternal hoe. The grass is turning yellow under his feet, the thistles multiply. The fire watcher will be lying on the ground and see the dusky face thrusting at him through the branches. As a rule he ignores the Arab, continues lying with his eyes on the sky. But sometimes he calls him and the man comes and kneels by his side, his heavy eyes wild with terror and hope. Perhaps he too will fail to convey anything and it will all remain dark.

The fire watcher talks to him therefore, quietly, reasonably, in a positively didactic manner. He tells him about the Crusades, and the other bends his head and absorbs the hard, alien words as one absorbing a melody. He tells him about the fervor, about the cruelty, about Jews committing suicide, about the Children's Crusade; things he has picked up from the books, the unfounded theories he has framed himself. His voice is warm, alive with imagination. The Arab listens with mounting tension and is filled with hate. When they return at twilight, lit by a soft autumnal glow, the fire watcher will lead the Arab to the tree-engulfed house and will linger a moment. Then the Arab explains something with hurried, confused gestures, squirming his severed tongue, tossing his head. He wishes to say that this is his house and that there used to be a village here as well and that they have simply hidden it all, buried it in the big forest.

The fire watcher looks on at this pantomime and his heart fills with joy. What is it that rouses such passion in the Arab? Apparently his wives have been murdered here as well. A dark affair, no doubt. Gradually he moves away, pretending not to understand. Did there used to be a village here? He sees nothing but trees.

More and more the Arab clings to him. They sit there, the three of them like a family, in the room on the second floor. The fire watcher sprawling on the bed, the child chained to the chair, the Arab crouching on the floor. Together they wait for the fire that does not come. The forest is dark and strong, a slow-growing world. These are his last days. His contract is drawing to an end. From time to time he gets up and throws one of the books back into the suitcase, startling the old Arab.

The nights are growing longer. Hot desert winds and rain-drops come. Tomorrow he will leave this place. He has discharged his duty faithfully. It isn't his fault that no fires have broken out. All the books are packed in the suitcase, scraps of paper litter the floor. The Arab has disappeared, has been missing since yesterday. The child is miserable. From time to time she raises her voice in a thin, ancient lament. The fire watcher is growing worried. At noon the Arab turns up suddenly. The child runs towards him but he takes no notice of her. He turns to the abdicating fire watcher instead, grabs him between two powerful hands and—feeble and soft that he is and suffering from a slight cold—impels him toward the edge of the observation post and explains whatever he can explain to him with no tongue. Perhaps he wishes to throw the abdicating fire watcher down two stories and into the forest. Perhaps he believes that only he, the fire watcher, can understand him. His eyes are burning. But the fire watcher is serene, unresponsive; he shadows his eyes with his palm, shrugs his shoulders, gives a meaningless little smile. What else is left him?

He collects his clothes and bundles them into the other suitcase.

Towards evening the Arab disappears again. The child has gone to look for him and has come back empty-handed. Gently the hours drift by. A single drop of rain. The fire watcher prepares supper and sets it before the child, but she cannot bring herself to eat. Like a little animal she scurries off once more into the forest to hunt for her father and returns in despair, by herself. Towards midnight she falls asleep at last. He undresses her and carries the shabby figure to the bed, covers it with the torn blanket. What a lonely woman she will grow to be. He muses. Something is flowing between his fingers, something like compassion. He lingers awhile. Then he returns to his observation post, sits on his chair, sleepy. Where will he be tomorrow? How about saying goodbye to the Fire Brigade? He picks up the receiver. Silence. The line is dead. Not a purr, not a gurgle. The sacred hush has invaded the wire as well.

He smiles contentedly. In the dark forest spread out before him the Arab is moving about like a silent dagger. He sits watching the world as one may watch a great play before the rising of the curtain. A little excitement, a little drowsing in one's seat. Midnight performance.

Then, suddenly—fire. Fire, unforeseen, leaping out of the corner. A long graceful flame. One tree is burning, a tree wrapped in prayer. For a long moment one tree is going through its hour of judgment and surrendering its spirit. He lifts the receiver. Yes, the line is dead. He is leaving here tomorrow.

The loneliness of a single flame in a big forest. He is beginning to worry whether the ground may not be too wet and the thistles too few, and the show be over after one flame. His eyes are closing. His drowsiness is greatest now, at this most wonderful of moments. He rises and starts pacing nervously through the room in order to walk off his fatigue. A short while passes and then a smile spreads over his face. He starts counting the flames. The Arab is setting the forest on fire at its four corners, then takes a firebrand and rushes through the trees like an evil spirit, setting fire to the rest. The thoroughness with which he goes about his task amazes the fire watcher. He goes down to look at the child. She is asleep. Back to the observation post—the forest is burning. He ought to run and raise the alarm, call for help. But his movements are so tranquil, his limbs leaden. Downstairs again. He adjusts the blanket over the child, pushes a lock of hair out of her eyes, goes back up, and a blast of hot air blows in his face. A great light out there. Five whole hills ablaze. Flames surge as in a frenzy high over the trees, roar at the lighted sky. Pines split and crash. Wild excitement sweeps him, rapture. He is happy. Where is the Arab now? The Arab speaks to him out of the fire, wishes to say everything, everything and at once. Will he understand?

Suddenly he is aware of another presence in the room. Swiftly he turns his head and sees the girl, half naked, eyes staring, the light of the fire playing over her face. He smiles and she weeps.

Intense heat wells up from the leisurely burning forest. The first excitement has passed. The fire is turning from a vision into a fact. Flames are mobilizing from all the four winds to come and visit the observation post. He ought to take his two suitcases and disappear. But he only takes the child. The lights of the neighboring settlements have become so pitiful, so plain. They are no doubt sure, over there, that the fight against the fire is already in full swing. Who would imagine that the fire is still being nourished here, brooded over? Hours will go by before the village watchmen come to wake the sleepers. The nights are already cold and people not disposed to throw off their blankets. He seizes the trembling child by the hand, goes down, and begins his retreat. The road is lit up till far into the distance. Behind his back the fire, and in his face a red, mad, burning moon that floats in the sky as though it wished to see the blaze as well. His head feels heavy, the road stretches ahead. They drag along, dipping in light and in darkness. In the lanes the trees whisper, agitated, waiting. A fearful rumor has reached them.

The observation post can be seen from afar, entirely lit up. The earth is casting its shackles. After a long walk the trees start thinning out at last, they grow smaller, then disappear. He arrives at the yellow waste, the wadi, his dream. A few dry, twisted trees, desert trees, alien and salty; trees that have sprung up parched, that the fire has no hold over. He sits the barefoot girl on the ground, slumps beside her. His exhaustion erupts within him and covers them both.

With sleeping eyes he sees the shining fire engines arrive at last, summoned by another. They too know that all is lost. In a dream the Arab appears—tired, disheveled, black with soot, his face ravaged—takes the child and vanishes. The fire watcher falls asleep, really asleep.

At dawn, shivering and damp, he emerges from the cover of the rocks, polishes his glasses and lo, he is the little scholar once more who has some kind of future before him. Five bare black hills, and slender wisps of blue-gray smoke rising from them. The observation post juts out over the bare landscape like a great demon grinning with white windows. For a moment it seems as though the forest had never burnt down but had simply pulled up its roots and gone off on a journey, far off on a journey, far off to the sea, for instance, which has suddenly come into view. The air is chilly. He adjusts his rumpled clothes, does up the last surviving button, rubs his hands to warm them, then treads softly among the smoking embers, light of foot. The first rays of the sun hit his bald patch. There is a sadness in this sudden nudity, the sadness of wars lost, blood shed in vain. Stately clouds sail in the cold sky. Soon the first rain will fall. He hears sounds of people everywhere. Utter destruction. Soot, a tangle of charred timber, its wounds still smoldering, and a residue of living branches unvisited by fire. Wherever he sets foot a thousand sparks fly. The commemorative plaques alone have survived; more than that, they have gained luster after their baptism of fire. There they lie, golden in the sun:

Louis Premington of Chicago, the King of Burundi and his People.

He enters the burnt building, climbs the charred stairs. Everything is still glowing hot. It is as though he were making his way through hell. He arrives at his room. The fire has visited it in his absence and held its riot of horror and glee. Shall we start with the books burnt to ashes? Or the contorted telephone? Or perhaps the binoculars melted to a lump? The map of the area has miraculously survived, is only blackened a bit at the edges. Gay fire kittens are still frolicking in the pillow and blankets. He turns his gaze to the fire smoking hills, frowns—there, out of the smoke and haze, the ruined village appears before his eyes; born anew in its basic outlines as an abstract drawing, as all things past and buried. He smiles to himself, a thin smile. Then abruptly it dies on his face. Directly under him, in the bluish abyss at the foot of the building, he sees the one in charge of forests who is edging his way to old age, wrapped in an old windbreaker, his face blue with cold. How has this one sprung up here all of a sudden?

The old one throws his gray head back and sends up a look full of hatred. Looking down upon the man from his high post, his own eyes would be faintly contemptuous in any case. For a few seconds they stay thus, with their eyes fixed on each other; at last the fire watcher gives his employer a fatuous smile of recognition and slowly starts coming down to him. the old man approaches him with quick mad steps. He would tear him to pieces if he could. He is near collapse with fury and pain. In a choking voice he demands the whole story, at once.

But there is no story, is there? There just isn't anything to tell. All there is, is: suddenly the fire sprang up. I lifted the receiver— the line was dead. That's it. The child had to be saved.

The rest is obvious. Yes, the fire watcher feels for the forest too. He has grown extremely attached to it during the spring, the summer, and half the autumn. So attached, in fact, that (to tell the truth for once) he hasn't managed to learn a single line.

He feels that the old man would like to sink to the ground and beat his head against some rock, would tear out the last of his white hair. The late fire watcher is surprised. Because the forests are insured, aren't they (at least ought to be, in his humble and practical opinion), and the fire won't be deducted from the budget of the old man's department, will it? Right now (this morning has found him amazingly clearheaded), he would very much like to be told about other forest fires. He is willing to bet that they were quite puny ones.

Except that now, ghostlike through the smoke, the firemen appear, accompanied by some fat and perspiring policemen. Soon he is surrounded by uniforms. Some of the men drop to the ground with exhaustion. Though the fire has not been completely tracked down as yet, they have already unearthed a startling piece of intelligence.

It has been arson.

Yes, arson. The smell of morning dew comes mingled with the smell of kerosene.

The old man is shattered.

"Arson?" he turns to the fire watcher.

But the other smiles gently.

The investigation is launched at once. First the firemen, who are supposed to write a report. They draw the fire watcher aside, take out large sheets of paper, ornate ballpoints, and then it appears that they have difficulty with the language, with phrasing and spelling. They are embarrassed. Tactfully he helps them, spells out words, formulates their sentences for them. They are very grateful.

"What have *you* lost in the fire?" they inquire sympathetically.

"Oh, nothing of importance. Some clothes and a few textbooks. Nothing to sorry about."

By the time they are through it is far into the morning. The Arab and the child appear from nowhere, led by two policemen. If he will be careful not to let his glance encounter those burning eyes he may possibly sleep in peace in the nights to come. Two tough-looking sergeants improvise a kind of emergency interrogation cell among the rocks, place him on a stone and start cross-examining him. For hours they persist, and that surprises him—the plodding tenacity, the diligence, page upon written page. A veritable research is being compiled before his eyes. The sun climbs to its zenith. He is hungry, thirsty. His interrogators chew enormous sandwiches and do not offer him a crumb. His glasses mist over with sweat. A queer autumn day. Inside the building they are conducting a simultaneous interrogation of the Arab, in Arabic eked out with gestures. Only the questions are audible.

The old forest manager dodges back and forth between the two interrogations, adding questions of his own, noting down replies. The interrogators have their subject with his back against the rock, they repeat the same questions over and over. A foul stench rises from the burnt forest, as though a huge carcass were rotting away all around them. The interrogation gains momentum. A big bore. What did he see, what did he hear, what did he do. It's insulting, this insistence upon the tangible—as though that were the main point, as though there weren't some idea involved here.

About noon his questioners change, two new ones appear and start the whole process over again. The subject is dripping with sweat. How humiliating, to be interrogated thus baldly on scorched earth, on rocks, after a sleepless night. The tedium of it. He spits, grows angry, loses his temper. He removes his glasses and his senses go numb. He starts contradicting himself. At three o'clock he breaks in their hands, is prepared to suggest the Arab as a possible clue.

This, of course, is what they have been waiting for. They had suspected the Arab all along. Promptly they handcuff him, and then all at once everything is wound up. The police drivers start their cars. The Arab is bundled into one of them and there is a gratified expression in his eyes now, a sense of achievement. The child clings to him desperately. Autumn clouds, autumn sadness, everything is flat and pointless. Suddenly he walks over to the forest manager and boldly demands a solution for the child. The other makes no reply. His old eyes wander over the lost forest as though in parting. This old man is going mad as well, his senses are growing confused. He stares at the fire watcher with vacant eyes as though he, too, had lost the words, as though he understood nothing. The fire watcher repeats his demand in a loud voice. The old man steps nearer.

"What?" he mumbles in a feeble voice, his eyes watery. Suddenly he throws himself at the fire watcher, attacks him with shriveled fists, hits out at him. With difficulty the firemen pull him back. To be sure, he blames only this one here. Yes, this one with the books, with the dim glasses, With that smug cynicism of his.

The policemen extricate the fire watcher and whisk him into one of their cars. They treat him toughly, something of the old man's hostility has stuck to them. Before he has time to say goodbye to the place where he has spent nearly six months he is being borne away at a mad pace towards town. They dump him on one of the side streets. He enters the first restaurant he comes to and gorges himself to the bursting point. Afterwards he paces the streets, bearded, dirty, sunburnt—a savage. The first dusty rain has already smirched the pavement.

At night, in some shabby hotel room, he is free to have a proper sleep, to sleep free from obligations for the first time, just sleep without any further dimensions. Except that he will not fall asleep, will only go on drowsing. Green forests will spring up before his troubled eyes. He may yet smart with sorrow and yearning, may feel constricted because he is shut in by four walls, not three.

And so it will be the day after, and perhaps all the days to come. The solitude has proved a success. True, his notes have been burned along with the books, but if anyone thinks that he does not remember—he does.

Yet he has become a stranger now in his so familiar town. He seems to have been forgotten already. A new generation is breaking into the circles. His waggish friends meet him, slap him on the back, and with ugly grins say, "We hear your forest burned down!" As we said, he is still young. But his real friends have given him up in despair. He drops in on them, on winter nights, shivering with cold—wet dog begging for fire and light—and they scowl and ask: "Well, what now?"

(1963)

—Translated by Miriam Arad

Nomad and Viper

∿

Amos Oz

1

The famine brought them.

They fled north from the horrors of famine, together with their dusty flocks. From September to April the desert had not known a moment's relief from drought. The loess was pounded to dust. Famine had spread through the nomads' encampments and wrought havoc among their flocks.

The military authorities gave the situation their urgent attention. Despite certain hesitations, they decided to open the roads leading north to the Bedouins. A whole population—men, women, and children—could not simply be abandoned to the horrors of starvation.

Dark, sinuous, and wiry, the desert tribesmen trickled along the dirt paths, and with them came their emaciated flocks. They meandered along gullies hidden from town-dwellers' eyes. A persistent stream pressed northward, circling the scattered settlements, staring wide-eyed at the sights of the settled land. The dark flocks spread into the fields of golden stubble, tearing and chewing with strong, vengeful teeth. The nomads' bearing was stealthy and subdued; they shrank from watchful eyes. They took pains to avoid encounters. Tried to conceal their presence.

If you passed them on a noisy tractor and set billows of dust loose on them, they would courteously gather their scattered flocks and give you a wide passage, wider by far than was necessary. They stared at you from a distance, frozen like statues. The scorching atmosphere blurred their appearance and gave a uniform look to their features: a shepherd with his staff, a woman with her babes, an old man with his eyes sunk deep in their sockets.

119

Some were half-blind, or perhaps feigned half-blindness from some vague alms-gathering motive. Inscrutable to the likes of you.

How unlike our well-tended sheep were their miserable specimens: knots of small, skinny beasts huddling into a dark, seething mass, silent and subdued, humble as their dumb keepers.

The camels alone spurn meekness. From atop tall necks they fix you with tired eyes brimming with scornful sorrow. The wisdom of age seems to lurk in their eyes, and a nameless tremor runs often through their skin.

Sometimes you manage to catch them unawares. Crossing a field on foot, you may suddenly happen on an indolent flock standing motionless, moon-struck, their feet apparently rooted in the parched soil. Among them lies the shepherd, fast asleep, dark as a block of basalt. You approach and cover him with a harsh shadow. You are startled to find his eyes wide open. He bares most of his teeth in a placatory smile. Some of them are gleaming, others decayed. His smell hits you. You grimace. Your grimace hits him like a punch in the face. Daintily he picks himself up, trunk erect, shoulders hunched. You fix him with a cold blue eye. He broadens his smile and utters a guttural syllable. His garb is a compromise: a short, patched European jacket over a white desert robe. He cocks his head to one side. An appeased gleam crosses his face. If you do not upbraid him, he suddenly extends his left hand and asks for a cigarette in rapid Hebrew. His voice has a silken quality, like that of a shy woman. If your mood is generous, you put a cigarette to your lips and toss another into his wrinkled palm. To your surprise, he snatches a gilt lighter from the recesses of his robe and offers a furtive flame. The smile never leaves his lips. His smile lasts too long, is unconvincing. A flash of sunlight darts off the thick gold ring adorning his finger and pierces your squinting eyes.

Eventually you turn your back on the nomad and continue on your way. After a hundred, two hundred paces, you may turn your head and see him standing just as he was, his gaze stabbing your back. You could swear that he is still smiling, that he will go on smiling for a long while to come.

And then, their singing in the night. A long-drawn-out, dolorous wail drifts on the night air from sunset until the early hours. The voices penetrate to the gardens and pathways of the kibbutz and charge our nights with an uneasy heaviness. No sooner have you settled down to sleep than a distant drumbeat sets the rhythm of your slumber like the pounding of an obdurate heart. Hot are the nights, and vapor-laden. Stray clouds caress the moon like a train of gentle camels, camels without any bells.

The nomads' tents are made up of dark drapes. Stray women drift around at night, barefoot and noiseless. Lean, vicious nomad hounds dart out of the camp to challenge the moon all night long. Their barking drives our kibbutz dogs insane. Our finest dog went mad one night, broke into the henhouse, and massacred the young chicks. It was not out of savagery that the watchmen shot him. There was no alternative. Any reasonable man would justify their action.

2

You might imagine that the nomad incursion enriched our heat-prostrated nights with a dimension of poetry. This may have been the case for some of our unattached girls. But we cannot refrain from mentioning a whole string of prosaic, indeed unaesthetic disturbances, such as hoof-and-mouth disease, crop damage, and an epidemic of petty thefts.

The hoof-and-mouth disease came out of the desert, carried by their livestock, which had never been subjected to any proper medical inspection. Although we took various early precautions, the virus infected our sheep and cattle, severely reducing the milk yield and killing off a number of animals.

As for the damage to the crops, we had to admit that we had never managed to catch one of the nomads in the act. All we ever found were the tracks of men and animals among the rows of vegetables, in the hayfields, and deep inside the carefully fenced orchards. And wrecked irrigation pipes, plot markers, farming implements left out in the fields, and other objects.

We are not the kind to take such things lying down. We are no believers in forbearance or vegetarianism. This is especially true of our younger men. Among the veteran founders there are a few adherents of Tolstoyan ideas and such like. Decency constrains me not to dwell in detail on certain isolated and exceptional acts of reprisal conducted by some of the youngsters whose patience had expired, such as cattle rustling, stoning a nomad boy, or beating one of the shepherds senseless. In defense of the perpetrators of the last-mentioned act of retaliation, I must state clearly that the shepherd in question had an infuriatingly sly face. He was blind in one eye, broken-nosed, drooling; and his mouth—on this the men responsible were unanimous—was set with long, curved fangs like a fox's. A man with such an appearance was capable of anything. And the Bedouins would certainly not forget this lesson.

The pilfering was the most worrisome aspect of all. They laid hands on the unripe fruit in our orchards, pocketed the faucets, whittled away piles of empty sacks in the fields, stole into the henhouses, and even made away with the modest valuables from our little houses.

The very darkness was their accomplice. Elusive as the wind, they passed through the settlement, evading both the guards we had posted and the extra guards we had added. Sometimes you would set out on a tractor or a battered jeep toward midnight to turn off the irrigation faucets in an outlying field and your headlights would trap fleeting shadows, a man or a night beast. An irritable guard decided one night to open fire, and in the dark he managed to kill a stray jackal.

Needless to say, the kibbutz secretariat did not remain silent. Several times Etkin, the secretary, called in the police, but their tracking dogs betrayed or failed them. Having led their handlers a few paces outside the kibbutz fence, they raised their black noses, uttered a savage howl, and stared foolishly ahead.

Spot raids on the tattered tents revealed nothing. It was as if the very earth had decided to cover up the plunder and brazenly outstare the victims. Eventually the elder of the tribe was brought to the kibbutz office, flanked by a pair of inscrutable nomads. The short-tempered policemen pushed them forward with repeated cries of *"Yallah, yallah."*

We, the members of the secretariat, received the elder and his men politely and respectfully. We invited them to sit down on the bench, smiled at them, and offered them steaming coffee prepared by Geula at Etkin's special request. The old man responded with elaborate courtesies, favoring us with a smile which he kept up from the beginning of the interview till its conclusion. He phrased his remarks in careful, formal Hebrew.

It was true that some of the youngsters of his tribe had laid hands on our property. Why should he deny it? Boys would be boys, and the world was getting steadily worse. He had the honor of begging our pardon and restoring the stolen property. Stolen property fastens its teeth in the flesh of the thief, as the proverb says. That was the way of it. What could one do about the hot-headedness of youth? He deeply regretted the trouble and distress we had been caused.

So saying, he put his hand into the folds of his robe and drew out a few screws, some gleaming, some rusty, a pair of pruning hooks, a stray knife-blade, a pocket flashlight, a broken hammer, and three grubby bank notes, as a recompense for our loss and worry.

Etkin spread his hands in embarrassment. For reasons best known to himself, he chose to ignore our guest's Hebrew and to reply in broken Arabic, the residue of his studies during the time of the riots and the siege. He opened his remarks with a frank and clear statement about the brotherhood of nations—the cornerstone of our ideology—and about the quality of neighborliness of which the people of the East had long been justly proud, and never more so than in these days of bloodshed and groundless hatred.

To Etkin's credit, let it be said that he did not shrink in the slightest from reciting a full and detailed list of the acts of theft, damage, and sabotage that our guest—as the result of oversight, no doubt—had refrained from mentioning in his apology. If all the stolen property were returned and the vandalism stopped once and for all, we would be wholeheartedly willing to open a new page in the relations of our two neighboring communities. Our children would doubtless enjoy and profit from an educational courtesy visit to the Bedouin encampment, the kind of visit that broadens horizons. And it went without saying that the tribe's children would pay a return visit to our kibbutz home, in the interest of deepening mutual understanding.

The old man neither relaxed nor broadened his smile, but kept it sternly at its former level as he remarked with an abundance of polite phrases that the gentlemen of the kibbutz would be able to prove no further thefts beyond those he had already admitted and for which he had sought our forgiveness.

He concluded with elaborate benedictions, wished us health and long life, posterity and plenty, then took his leave and departed, accompanied by his two barefooted companions wrapped in their dark robes. They were soon swallowed up by the wadi that lay outside the kibbutz fence.

Since the police had proved ineffectual—and had indeed abandoned the investigation—some of our young men suggested making an excursion one night to teach the savages a lesson in a language they would really understand.

Etkin rejected their suggestion with disgust and with reasonable arguments. The young men, in turn, applied to Etkin a number of epithets that decency obliges me to pass over in silence. Strangely enough, Etkin ignored their insults and reluctantly agreed to put their suggestion before the kibbutz secretariat. Perhaps he was afraid that they might take matters into their own hands.

Toward evening, Etkin went around from room to room and invited the committee to an urgent meeting at eight-thirty. When he came to Geula, he told her about the young men's ideas and the undemocratic pressure to which he was being subjected, and asked her to bring along to the meeting a pot of black coffee and a lot of good will. Geula responded with an acid smile. Her eyes were bleary because Etkin had awakened her from a troubled sleep. As she changed her clothes, the night fell, damp and hot and close.

3

Damp and close and hot the night fell on the kibbutz, tangled in the dust-laden cypresses, oppressed the lawns and ornamental shrubs. Sprinklers scattered water onto the thirsty lawn, but it was swallowed up at once: perhaps it evaporated even before it touched the grass. An irritable phone rang vainly in the locked office. The walls of the houses gave out a damp vapor. From the kitchen chimney a stiff column of smoke rose like an arrow into the heart of the sky, because there was no breeze. From the greasy sinks came a shout. A dish had been broken and somebody was bleeding. A fat house cat had killed a lizard or a snake and dragged its prey onto the baking concrete path to toy with it lazily in the dense evening sunlight. An ancient tractor started to rumble in one of the sheds, choked, belched a stench of oil, roared, sputtered, and finally managed to set out to deliver an evening meal to the second shift, who were toiling in an outlying field. Near the Persian Lilac Geula saw a bottle dirty with the remains of a greasy liquid. She kicked at it repeatedly, but instead of shattering, the bottle rolled heavily among the rosebushes. She picked up a big stone. She tried to hit the bottle. She longed to smash it. The stone missed. The girl began to whistle a vague tune.

Geula was a short, energetic girl of twenty-nine or so. Although she had not yet found a husband, none of us would deny her good qualities, such as the dedication she lavished on local social and cultural activities. Her face was pale and thin. No one could rival her in brewing strong coffee—coffee to raise the dead, we called it. A pair of bitter lines were etched at the corners of her mouth.

On summer evenings, when the rest of us would lounge in a group on a rug spread on one of the lawns and launch jokes and bursts of cheerful song heavenward, accompanied by clouds of cigarette smoke, Geula would shut herself up in her room and not join us until she had prepared the pot of scalding, strong coffee. She it was, too, who always took pains to ensure that there was no shortage of biscuits.

What had passed between Geula and me is not relevant here, and I shall make do with a hint or two. Long ago we used to stroll together to the orchards in the evening and talk. It was all a long time ago, and it is a long time since it ended. We would exchange unconventional political ideas or argue about the latest books. Geula was a stern and sometimes merciless critic: I was covered in confusion. She did not like my stories, because of the extreme polarity of situations, scenery, and characters, with no intermediate shades between black and white. I would utter an apology or a denial but Geula always had ready proofs and she was a very methodical thinker. Sometimes I would dare to rest a conciliatory hand on her neck, and wait for her to calm down. But she never relaxed completely. If once or twice she leaned against me, she always blamed her broken sandal or her aching head. And so we drifted apart. To this day she still cuts my stories out of the periodicals, and arranges them in a cardboard box kept in a special drawer devoted to them alone.

I always buy her a new book of poems for her birthday. I creep into her room when she is out and leave the book on her table, without any inscription or dedication. Sometimes we happen to sit together in the dining hall. I avoid her glance, so as not to have to face her mocking madness. On hot days, when faces are covered in sweat, the acne on her cheeks reddens and she seems to have no hope. When the cool of autumn comes, I sometimes find her pretty and attractive from a distance. On such days Geula likes to walk to the orchards in the early evening. She goes alone and comes back alone. Some of the youngsters come and ask me what she is looking for there, and they have a malicious snicker on their faces. I tell them that I don't know. And I really don't.

4

Viciously Geula picked up another stone to hurl at the bottle. This time she did not miss, but she still failed to hear the shattering sound she craved. The stone grazed the bottle, which tinkled faintly, and disappeared under one of the bushes. A third stone, bigger and heavier than the other two, was launched from ridiculously close range: the girl trampled on the loose soil of the flower bed and stood right over the bottle. This time there was a harsh, dry explosion, which brought no relief. Must get out.

Damp and close and hot the night fell, its heat pricking the skin like broken glass. Geula retraced her steps, passed the balcony of her room, tossed her sandals inside, and walked down barefoot onto the dirt path.

The clods of earth tickled the soles of her feet. There was a rough friction, and her nerve endings quivered with flickers of vague excitement. Beyond the rocky hill the shadows were waiting for her: the orchard in the last of the light. With determined hands she widened the gap in the fence and slipped through. At that moment a slight evening breeze began to stir. It was a warmish summer breeze with no definite direction. An old sun rolled westward, trying to be sucked up by the dusty horizon. A last tractor climbed back to the depot, panting along the dirt road from the outlying plots. No doubt it was the tractor that had taken the second-shift workers their supper. It seemed shrouded in smoke or summer haze.

Geula bent down and picked some pebbles out of the dust. Absently she began to throw them back again, one by one. There were lines of poetry on her lips, some by the young poets she was fond of, others her own. By the irrigation pipe she paused, bent down, and drank as though kissing the faucet. But the faucet was rusty, the pipe was still hot, and the water was tepid and foul. Nevertheless she bent her head and let the water pour over her face and neck and into her shirt. A sharp taste of rust and wet dust filled her throat. She closed her eyes and stood in silence. No relief. Perhaps a cup of coffee. But only after the orchard. Must go now.

5

The orchards were heavily laden and fragrant. The branches intertwined, converging above the rows of trunks to form a shadowy dome. Underfoot the irrigated soil retained a hidden dampness. Shadows upon shadows at the foot of those gnarled trunks. Geula picked a plum, sniffed and crushed it. Sticky juice dripped from it. The sight made her feel dizzy. And the smell. She crushed a second plum. She picked another and rubbed it on her cheek till she was spattered with juice. Then, on her knees, she picked up a dry stick and scratched shapes in the dust. Aimless lines and curves. Sharp angles. Domes. A distant bleating invaded the orchard. Dimly she became aware of a sound of bells. She was far away. The nomad stopped behind Geula's back, as silent as a phantom. He dug at the dust with his big toe, and his shadow fell in front of him. But the girl was blinded by a flood of sounds. She saw and heard nothing. For a long time she continued to kneel on the ground and draw shapes in the dust with her twig. The nomad waited patiently in total silence. From time to time he closed his good eye and stared ahead of him with the other, the blind one. Finally he reached out and bestowed a long caress on the air. His obedient shadow moved in the dust. Geula stared, leapt to her feet, and leaned against the nearest tree, letting out a low sound. The nomad let his shoulders drop and put on a faint smile. Geula raised her arm and stabbed the air with her twig. The nomad continued to smile. His gaze dropped to her bare feet. His voice was hushed, and the Hebrew he spoke exuded a rare gentleness:

"What time is it?"

Geula inhaled to her lungs' full capacity. Her features grew sharp, her glance cold. Clearly and dryly she replied: "It is half past six. Precisely."

The Arab broadened his smile and bowed slightly, as if to acknowledge a great kindness. "Thank you very much, miss."

His bare toe had dug deep into the damp soil, and clods of earth crawled at his feet as if there were a startled mole burrowing underneath them.

Geula fastened the top button of her blouse. There were large perspiration stains on her shirt, drawing attention to her armpits. She could smell the sweat on her body, and her nostrils widened. The nomad closed his blind eye and looked up. His good eye blinked. His skin was very dark; it was alive and warm. Creases were etched in his cheeks. He was unlike any man Geula had ever known, and his smell and color and breathing were also strange. His nose was long and narrow, and a shadow of a mustache showed beneath it. His cheeks seemed to be sunk into his mouth cavity. His lips were thin and fine, much finer than her own. But the chin was strong, almost expressing contempt or rebellion.

The man was repulsively handsome, Geula decided to herself. Unconsciously she responded with a mocking half-smile to the nomad's persistent grin. The Bedouin drew two crumpled cigarettes from a hidden pocket in his belt, laid them on his dark, outstretched palm, and held them out to her as though proffering crumbs to a sparrow. Geula dropped her smile, nodded twice, and accepted one. She ran the cigarette through her fingers, slowly, dreamily, ironing out the creases, straightening it, and only then did she put it to her lips. Quick as lightning, before she realized the purpose of the man's sudden movement, a tiny flame was dancing in front of her. Geula shielded the lighter with her hand even though there was no breeze in the orchard, sucked in the flame, closed her eyes. The nomad lit his own cigarette and bowed politely.

"Thank you very much," he said in his velvety voice.

"Thanks," Geula replied. "Thank you."

"You from the kibbutz?"

Geula nodded.

"Goo-d." An elongated syllable escaped from between his gleaming teeth. "That's goo-d."

The girl eyed his desert robe.

"Aren't you hot in that thing?"

The man gave an embarrassed, guilty smile, as if he had been caught red-handed. He took a slight step backward.

"Heaven forbid, it's not hot. Really not. Why? There's air, there's water . . . " And he fell silent.

The treetops were already growing darker. A first jackal sniffed the oncoming night and let out a tired howl. The orchard filled with a scurry of small, busy feet. All of a sudden Geula became aware of the throngs of black goats intruding in search of their master. They swirled silently in and out of the fruit trees. Geula pursed her lips and let out a short whistle of surprise.

"What are you doing here, anyway? Stealing?"

The nomad cowered as though a stone had been thrown at him. His hand beat a hollow tattoo on his chest.

"No, not stealing, heaven forbid, really not." He added a lengthy oath in his own language and resumed his silent smile. His blind eye winked nervously. Meanwhile an emaciated goat darted forward and rubbed against his leg. He kicked it away and continued to swear with passion:

"Not steal, truly, by Allah no steal. Forbidden to steal."

"Forbidden in the Bible," Geula replied with a dry, cruel smile. "Forbidden to steal, forbidden to kill, forbidden to covet, and forbidden to commit adultery. The righteous are above suspicion."

The Arab cowered before the onslaught of words and looked down at the ground. Shamefaced. Guilty. His foot continued to kick restlessly at the loose earth. He was trying to ingratiate himself. His blind eye narrowed. Geula was momentarily alarmed: surely it was a wink. The smile left his lips. He spoke in a soft, drawn-out whisper, as though uttering a prayer.

"Beautiful girl, truly very beautiful girl. Me, I got no girl yet. Me still young. No girl yet. Yaaa," he concluded with a guttural yell directed at an impudent goat that had rested its forelegs against a tree trunk and was munching hungrily at the foliage. The animal cast a pensive, skeptical glance at its master, shook its beard, and solemnly resumed its munching.

Without warning, and with amazing agility, the shepherd leapt through the air and seized the beast by the hindquarters, lifted it above his head, let out a terrifying, savage screech, and flung it ruthlessly to the ground. Then he spat and turned to the girl.

"Beast," he apologized. "Beast. What to do. No brains. No manners."

The girl let go of the tree trunk against which she had been resting and leaned toward the nomad. A sweet shudder ran down her back. Her voice was still firm and cool.

"Another cigarette?" she asked. "Have you got another cigarette?"

The Bedouin replied with a look of anguish, almost of despair. He apologized. He explained at length that he had no more cigarettes, not even one, not even a little one. No more. All gone. What a pity. He would gladly, very gladly, have given her one. None left. All gone.

The beaten goat was getting shakily to its feet. Treading circumspectly, it returned to the tree trunk, disingenuously observing its master out of the corner of its eye. The shepherd watched it without moving. The goat reached up, rested its front hooves on the tree, and calmly continued munching. The Arab picked up a heavy stone and swung his arm wildly. Geula seized his arm and restrained him.

"Leave it. Why? Let it be. It doesn't understand. It's only a beast. No brains, no manners."

The nomad obeyed. In total submission he let the stone drop. Then Geula let go of his arm. Once again the man drew the lighter out of his belt. With thin, pensive fingers he toyed with it. He accidentally lit a small flame, and hastily blew at it. The flame widened slightly, slanted, and died. Nearby a jackal broke into a loud, piercing wail. The rest of the goats, meanwhile, had followed the example of the first and were absorbed in rapid, almost angry munching.

A vague wail came from the nomad encampment away to the south, the dim drum beating time to its languorous call. The dusky men were sitting around their campfires, sending skyward their single-noted song. The night took up the strain and answered with dismal cricket-chirp. Last glimmers of light were dying away in the far west. The orchard stood in darkness. Sounds gathered all around, the wind's whispering, the goats' sniffing, the rustle of ravished leaves. Geula pursed her lips and whistled an old tune. The nomad listened to her with rapt attention, his head cocked to one side in surprise, his mouth hanging slightly open. She glanced at her watch. The hands winked back at her with a malign, phosphorescent glint, but said nothing. Night.

The Arab turned his back on Geula, dropped to his knees, touched his forehead on the ground, and began mumbling fervently.

"You've got no girl yet," Geula broke into his prayer. "You're still too young." Her voice was loud and strange. Her hands were on her hips, her breathing still even. The man stopped praying, turned his dark face toward her, and muttered a phrase in Arabic. He was still crouched on all fours, but his pose suggested a certain suppressed joy.

"You're still young," Geula repeated, "very young. Perhaps twenty. Perhaps thirty. Young. No girl for you. Too young."

The man replied with a very long and solemn remark in his own language. She laughed nervously, her hands embracing her hips.

"What's the matter with you?" she inquired, laughing still. "Why are you talking to me in Arabic all of a sudden? What do you think I am? What do you want here anyway?"

Again the nomad replied in his own language. Now a note of terror filled his voice. With soft, silent steps he recoiled and withdrew as though from a dying creature. She was breathing heavily now, panting, trembling. A single wild syllable escaped from the shepherd's mouth: a sign between him and his goats. The goats responded and thronged around him, their feet pattering on the carpet of dead leaves like cloth ripping. The crickets fell silent. The goats huddled in the dark, a terrified, quivering mass, and disappeared into the darkness, the shepherd vanishing in their midst.

Afterward, alone and trembling, she watched an airplane passing in the dark sky above the treetops, rumbling dully, its lights blinking alternately with a rhythm as precise as that of the drums: red, green, red, green, red. The night covered over the traces. There was a smell of bonfires on the air and a smell of dust borne on the breeze. Only a slight breeze among the fruit trees. Then panic struck her and her blood froze. Her mouth opened to scream but she did not scream; she started to run and she ran barefoot with all her strength for home and stumbled and rose and ran as though pursued, but only the sawing of the crickets chased after her.

6

She returned to her room and made coffee for all the members of the secretariat, because she remembered her promise to Etkin. Outside the cool of evening had set in, but inside her room the walls were hot and her body was also on fire. Her clothes stuck to her body because she had been running, and her armpits disgusted her. The spots on her face were glowing. She stood and counted the number of times the coffee boiled—seven successive boilings, as she had learned to do it from her brother Ehud before he was killed in a reprisal raid in the desert. With pursed lips she counted as the black liquid rose and subsided, rose and subsided, bubbling fiercely as it reached its climax.

That's enough, now. Take clean clothes for the evening. Go to the showers.

What can that Etkin understand about savages. A great socialist. What does he know about Bedouins. A nomad sniffs out weakness from a distance. Give him a kind word, or a smile, and he pounces on you like a wild beast and tries to rape you. It was just as well I ran away from him.

In the showers the drain was clogged and the bench was greasy. Geula put her clean clothes on the stone ledge. I'm not shivering because the water's cold. I'm shivering with disgust. Those black fingers, and how he went straight for my throat. And his teeth. And the goats. Small and skinny like a child, but so strong. It was only by biting and kicking that I managed to escape. Soap my belly and everything, soap it again and again. Yes, let the boys go right away tonight to their camp and smash their black bones because of what they did to me. Now I must get outside.

7

She left the shower and started back toward her room, to pick up the coffee and take it to the secretariat. But on the way she heard crickets and laughter, and she remembered him bent down on all fours, and she was alarmed and stood still in the dark. Suddenly she vomited among the flowering shrubs. And she began to cry. Then her knees gave way. She sat down to rest on the dark earth. She stopped crying. But her teeth continued to chatter, from the cold or from pity. Suddenly she was not in a hurry anymore, even the coffee no longer seemed important, and she thought to herself: There's still time. There's still time.

Those planes sweeping the sky tonight were probably on a night-bombing exercise. Repeatedly they roared among the stars, keeping up a constant flashing, red, green, red, green, red. In counterpoint came the singing of the nomads and their drums, a persistent heartbeat in the distance: One, one, two, One, one, two. And silence.

8

From eight-thirty until nearly nine o'clock we waited for Geula. At five to nine Etkin said that he could not imagine what had happened; he could not recall her ever having missed a meeting or been late before; at all events, we must now begin the meeting and turn to the business on the agenda.

He began with a summary of the facts. He gave details of the damage that had apparently been caused by the Bedouins, although there was no formal proof, and enumerated the steps that had been taken on the committee's initiative. The appeal to good will. Calling in the police. Strengthening the guard around the settlement. Tracking dogs. The meeting with the elders of the tribe. He had to admit, Etkin said, that we had now reached an impasse. Nevertheless, he believed that we had to maintain a sense of balance and not give way to extremism, because hatred always gave rise to further hatred. It was essential to break the vicious circle of hostility. He therefore opposed with all the moral force at his disposal the approach—and particularly the intentions—of certain of the younger members. He wished to remind us, by way of conclusion, that the conflict between herdsmen and tillers of the soil was as old as human civilization, as seemed to be evidenced by the story of Cain, who rose up against Abel, his brother. It was fitting, in view of the social gospel we had adopted, that we should put an end to this ancient feud, too, just as we had put an end to other ugly phenomena. It was up to us, and everything depended on our moral strength.

The room was full of tension, even unpleasantness. Rami twice interrupted Etkin and on one occasion went so far as to use the ugly word "rubbish." Etkin took offense, accused the younger members of planning terrorist activities, and said in conclusion, "We're not going to have that sort of thing here."

Geula had not arrived, and that was why there was no one to cool down the temper of the meeting. And no coffee. A heated exchange broke out between me and Rami. Although in age I be-longed with the younger men, I did not agree with their propos-als. Like Etkin, I was absolutely opposed to answering the nomads with violence—for two reasons, and when I was given permission to speak I mentioned them both. In the first place, nothing really serious had happened so far. A little stealing perhaps, but even that was not certain: every faucet or pair of pliers that a tractor driver left in a field or lost in the garage or took home with him was immediately blamed on the Bedouins. Secondly, there had been no rape or murder. Hereupon Rami broke in excitedly and asked what I was waiting for. Was I perhaps waiting for some small incident of rape that Geula could write poems about and I could make into a short story? I flushed and cast around in my mind for a telling retort.

But Etkin, upset by our rudeness, immediately deprived us both of the right to speak and began to explain his position all over again. He asked us how it would look if the papers reported that a kibbutz had sent out a lynch mob to settle scores with its Arab neighbors. As Etkin uttered the phrase "lynch mob" Rami made a gesture to his young friends that is commonly used by bas-ketball players. At this signal they rose in a body and walked out in disgust, leaving Etkin to lecture to his heart's content to three el-derly women and a long-retired member of Parliament.

After a moment's hesitation I rose and followed them. True, I did not share their views, but I, too—in an arbitrary and insulting manner—had been deprived of the right to speak.

9

If only Geula had come to the meeting and brought her famous coffee with her, it is possible that tempers might have been soothed. Perhaps, too, her understanding might have achieved some sort of compromise between the conflicting points of view. But the coffee was standing, cold by now, on the table in her room. And Geula herself was lying among the bushes behind the Memorial Hall, watching the lights of the planes and listening to the sounds of the night. How she longed to make her peace and to forgive. Not to hate him and wish him dead. Perhaps to get up and go to him, to find him among the wadis and forgive him and never come back. Even to sing to him. The sharp slivers piercing her skin and drawing blood were the fragments of the bottle she had smashed here with a big stone at the beginning of the evening. And the living thing slithering among the slivers of glass among the clods of earth was a snake, perhaps a venomous snake, perhaps a viper. It stuck out a forked tongue, and its triangular head was cold and erect. Its eyes were dark glass. It could never close them, because it had no eyelids. A thorn in her flesh, perhaps a sliver of glass. She was very tired. And the pain was vague, almost pleasant. A distant ringing in her ears. To sleep now. Wearily through the thickening film, she watched the gang of youngsters crossing the lawn on their way to the fields and the wadi to even the score with the nomads. We were carrying short, thick sticks. Excitement was dilating our pupils. And the blood was drumming in our temples.

Far away in the darkened orchards stood somber, dust-laden cypresses, swaying to and fro with a gentle religious fervor. She felt tired, and that was why she did not come to see us off. But her fingers caressed the dust, and her face was very calm and almost beautiful.

(1963)

—Translated by Nicholas de Lange

Excerpt from
Refuge

༅

SAMI MICHAEL

Chapter 4

Magid charmed the townspeople of Jenin. They said, in the coffeehouses, that his smile instantly calmed all their fears. Tough guys who would rather face a loaded pistol than a syringe had nothing but praise for Magid, especially for his cunning way of keeping the syringes out of sight, he himself liked to tell comic stories about it. He and the poet were sitting in the dentist's living room, waiting for Abla to return from some Party meeting. She was a teacher, and on Fridays, when schools were closed, she would see to most of her Party duties. The dentist smiled over his cup of coffee.

"One day," he recalled, "a well-known hoodlum from Nablus came into the clinic, a guy who would kill for a penny. His mug would scare you more than a pair of extracting tongs. Well, his mouth was so swollen he had trouble speaking. He came in, grabbed the patient who was in the chair, and threw him out. I was boiling mad. The patient he had thrown out was a sensitive type, Abla's uncle. But once this hoodlum sat himself down in the chair, his courage immediately failed him, and his eyes rolled in terror. I told him I couldn't pull the tooth because of the awful infection. 'Pull it out!' he yelled. I came close, examined him, and again and again told him it was impossible. But now I couldn't get away from the chair. The bastard grabbed my balls and roared, 'Now I've got your life in my hands and you've got mine in yours. And no lousy injections, either.' Fatkhi, he was ready to butcher me. So I said to myself, as Allah is great, I'll screw this gangster once and for all. 'It isn't just one tooth,' I lied to him. 'Never mind,' he shouted, 'start pulling, and like I told you, no needles!' I said to him: 'You know

135

what? Why don't you inject me, so you'll see it's not as terrible as you think. Then I'll inject you.' He liked the idea. I guided his free hand—the one on my balls didn't relax for a second—and he stuck the syringe into my jaw. He must have considered me either a hero or a magician. Then it was my turn. I jabbed him, Fatkhi, I jabbed and jabbed until his mouth was just a block of wood, and then I started in with a vengeance. I ripped out half of his teeth to make sure he wouldn't have many more opportunities to visit me. But do you know what? That murderer, who can hardly chew anything today, thinks I did him a great favor. Every month or two he's here. You see that box of grapes over there? He brought it just this morning from Nablus."

The poet grinned. "I'll bet he lifted it from some poor grocer."

"Fatkhi, you should know this—when a murderer wants to give you a gift, he doesn't steal it. He pays good money for it."

Fatkhi grinned again. "Not a bad idea, grabbing your balls—what a pair of hostages!"

Magid became serious. "You use the same tactics, my friend."

"How's that?" The poet was astonished. "Me?"

"You count on our friendship to force me to lie to the Party, man."

"I had to come, Magid."

"You've disobeyed orders, and now I'm in cahoots with you, against my will."

The maid was collecting the coffee cups. She stole several glances at the handsome poet and them minced light-footedly from the room. "That piece is from the camp," the dentist said. "She's in love with you already."

"Be serious, Magid."

"All right, I won't report on this visit. But if it gets out, we'll both be in the same boat, sweetheart."

"I don't care."

"Allah! Allah!" Magid cried. "What, have you had enough of life among the conquerors? I've heard your nights in Tel Aviv aren't as boring as all that. And you're engaged to a real beauty. What else do you want, Fatkhi? Are you bored?" The dentist knew that this wasn't so. Deep in his heart, however, Fatkhi thought he was sneering at him.

Abla arrived. Her face radiated shrewdness, and her shapely body made up in part for her homeliness. "Fatkhi," she cried, in the tone of an unself-conscious woman. "How many boats did you lose at sea today? You look so miserable!"

"Magid is persecuting me."

"He's a professional sadist."

"I speak to him in all seriousness and he tells me to go to Tel Aviv."

"Don't pay any attention to him. It's only jealousy—the pure jealousy of a man who used to live in a refugee camp. The money may pour down like rain, but at heart Magid will always be a refugee."

"Actually," Magid said, "I am at peace with myself. You're not fair, Abla. I buried the refugee inside me. It's been years since he gave up the ghost."

"Every day you strangle him to death, and the next day he comes back to life. Whenever you're asked where you come from, you still say Jaffa."

Her husband smiled. "And you?"

"From Ramle," she laughed.

"Although she was born here, in Jenin."

Fatkhi knew that every child in the refugee camps learned to respond this way when asked where he was from.

"Have the children eaten?" Abla asked.

"They ate and they're playing outside," her husband answered. "And we're dying of hunger."

"How can you have any appetite after poking around in so many stinking mouths?" she teased him. "Besides, you're getting as pot-bellied as a shopkeeper and as bald as a druggist, Magid. Look at how Fatkhi keeps his great figure."

The poet was perturbed, but Magid joked, "That's his second weapon in Tel Aviv."

"And what's his first?"

"Poetry."

Abla laughed and turned serious. "In connection with the Party?"

"No," the poet answered. "A personal problem."

"Listen . . . "

"Abla," her husband interrupted. "I've already told him, I've explained to him a hundred times that Zuheir can't solve other people's personal problems now."

"That's right." She looked clear-eyed at the poet. Abla was one of the few women in Jenin who dared to look a man right in the eyes. "Zuheir's changed. He's like another man since the Jews pardoned him."

"But I want to see him."

Abla was annoyed by his childish stubbornness. "We've told you that Zuheir isn't Zuheir anymore. I don't know if he'll be willing to meet you. He stays in Kabatiye, and when people come to see him he makes it plain that they're not wanted."

"Is he sick?" the poet asked.

"He's another man," the woman said vaguely, without going into detail. "And he refuses to be shaken out of it."

"I've got a Jewish friend," Fatkhi said. "A revolutionary from birth. He sat in jail for years. His name is Marduch. Once we had a talk about ex-prisoners . . . He said that there were all kinds. The strangest ones are those who were on the point of breaking but didn't break. They start to fold up inside. They close all their shutters. They tremble at the idea that they might have to relive their experiences . . . "

Abla, hearing this, furrowed her narrow brow and took her upper lip between her teeth. Under her nostrils a hairy little track sprouted. "I'm not as smart as you and I'm no great expert in psychology. But when you look at Zuheir you get the feeling that it's not only his hands that are trembling. Something inside him is shaking . . . " She added mysteriously, "It's not fear, it's more like the way a car shakes and vibrates when it's about to go off the road."

Magid wiped his glasses with a handkerchief. "Maybe," he said thoughtfully, "maybe they ought to meet. They'd pour out their troubles to each other."

Again Abla took her lip between her tiny teeth. "And what are your problems?" she asked the poet.

"I can't find myself," he said, and immediately regretted his frankness.

"You can't find yourself?" she marveled, without the slightest sympathy. "But you're to be found everywhere. Even in Beirut."

"In Beirut?" The poet was bewildered.

"It seems you haven't seen the latest issue of *Al-Adib*."

The poet shook his head.

"Abla!" Magid said.

"You're not doing him any favor," she answered. "Why hide things from him?" and she went to the bookcase and took out the magazine.

The couple left him sitting in the armchair. The magazine was heavy in his arms and he let it drop onto his knees, and as he did so it seemed to pull his head and shoulders down with it. The open window darkened in the afternoon light and the town outside seemed to die. The house was perfectly still. In his ears the poet, like a deep-sea diver, felt a growing, painful pressure. He had discovered an act of treachery, and his lips murmured the reproach of a lover betrayed—No, Fakhri, no! His anger had not yet come flooding over him. Made up himself of layer upon layer of rage and hatred, the poet could not be angry with his one and only childhood friend, his friend since he had been weaned from his mother's breast. No, Fakhri, no! he moaned, and the pressure in his ears grew.

Just yesterday it was, a few weeks ago, or perhaps several months had gone by already—oh hell, the time wasn't important—they had sat on one bed in Moscow like two high school girls, spilling out their hearts. There had always been this rapport between them, free and pure. Fakhri had said that he would not return to Israel on a Party assignment, he had had enough of the fetters of discipline and yearned to rid himself of all the stains of Israel that were on him. He was going to travel by way of Damascus to Beirut, where he would find his place in the Palestine Liberation Organization. They were both stirred. That Moscow evening was clouded by the poet's impending separation from his friend, the literary critic who esteemed him so highly. "We'll meet again somehow," they pledged one another, like a young girl and a soldier on a railway station platform.

And thus, in the pages of this literary magazine, his bosom friend sends him greetings: "A traitor slipping craftily into the enemy's lap . . . a poet who casts his insipid verse before the murderers of his people . . . an intellectual whore fallen into captivity in the parlors of the poison-mongers . . . "

No, Fakhri, no.

Unreasonably, hoping against hope, he looked again at the byline. Maybe he'd lost his mind. Maybe his eyes deceived him, he thought, even though he knew beyond doubt that this was his friend's flashy style. "The spiritual murder of a People." And under the title: "by Fakhri Biadsah."

No, Fakhri . . .

There was a sound of dishes and knives and forks being set on the table. Now he became aware of Abla's clear voice: "Fatkhi, come and eat."

The poet raised his shrouded eyes to the open window, as if meaning to leap through it into the silent afternoon streets, and beyond them to the brown fields and the horizon . . . as if he wished to flee all the way back there. When he realized what "there" meant, he trembled. There meant Israel, the Israel he hated.

Magid's comforting voice sounded through the open door. "*Ya Sheik,* come and eat already. You're a creative artist, you should be used to falling down and getting slapped in the face."

He left the living room, the magazine still in his hand. He approached the table and dropped into a chair. The paper rustled on his knees. "Fakhri," he murmured.

"He got you good!" Abla said merrily, her eyes sparkling beneath her narrow forehead.

"You don't understand," the poet stammered.

"But you signed—isn't it true that you signed? So what are you getting excited about?"

"When their children were killed on that bus, all hell broke loose. Here you work single-mindedly, Abla, and you forget our problems. You forget that we're caught between the hammer and the anvil. We work among Jews. I envy you. I envy Fakhri. How easy it is for him to say whatever comes into his head, sitting in Beirut. Don't forget that in Israel the Party itself is made up of Jews and Arabs: We have to keep them in mind. When they demanded that we express our regret over the death of those children, when they demanded that we condemn that action, we turned around and demanded that they condemn the Israeli army's aggression in Lebanon, and they agreed."

"The death of the children," Abla murmured. "In your statement it said, 'The murder of the children.' We're murderers in your eyes, Fatkhi. Go and explain that to Zuheir."

Magid concentrated on his food. From time to time he cast a smiling glance at the poet, who was preparing to repel Abla's assault.

"I will explain it to Zuheir! And how!" The poet was afire with emotion, not to his advantage.

Abla tore at her food. "You mentioned your Jewish friend. What did you say his name was?"

"Marduch."

"Does he also make you walk the tightrope between the thieves and their victims?"

"He was shocked. As far as he's concerned, children are children. He has only one child himself, a retarded child. Fathers like that are crazy about anything having to do with children. If I lived here permanently, things would look simpler to me."

The woman refused to let up on him. "When do you envy us—when you go to Moscow, or when you go to Tel Aviv?"

"Abla!" Magid cried. "Let the poor man eat."

"I don't know," the poet answered evenly. "I'm an outsider in Tel Aviv. In a certain way I'm an outsider in my village, too. I come here and visit the refugee camp, and I'm an outsider here as well. I'm a stranger, Abla, a stranger in my own country."

Revolutionary women detest agonizing, especially in men. She promptly assumed an even more judgmental tone. "The Jews have turned your head, sweetheart. You're so taken up with them that you've forgotten that you're a member of the Party. You go into the refugee camp in a coat and tie and you want them to bow down to you. You've forgotten that there's still a class war being fought in the world."

Fatkhi had no more stomach for this conversation. "Will I see Zuheir?"

Magid smiled good-naturedly. "You seem to be very sure that he'll solve your problems."

"Will I see him?"

"All right," the dentist agreed. "Go rest now. Abla's spoiled your appetite."

Fatkhi went off to the living room. One wall was completely covered with books. He leafed through several and then dropped into the armchair. It was not only his appetite that Abla had spoiled. She had hurt his manly pride. And she had done it intentionally. No female made fun of him like that. He remembered their first encounter well. She had gazed at him, stared at his clear face and green eyes. Her shapely body twisted and her face became homelier than ever. He had thrown her a gallant smile. She warded it off, and immediately closed herself off to him.

Since bursting forth from his village, Fatkhi had been with many women, all kinds of women, but the ones who closed themselves off always frightened him. In time he adjusted to the strange behavior of strange women, convinced that these were usually women saddled with impotent husbands, who feared that Fatkhi would notice the hunger in their eyes. They always behaved aggressively. And in those few who finally let their guard down, aggression changed into the most frightful self-abasement.

Abla is famished, he decided vindictively. He stretched out his legs on the floor polished by the maid from the camp, and hung his head back. A light breeze fluttered the curtain behind him and a bird chirped on the branch of the pomegranate tree outside. Suddenly he relaxed. A smile came to his lips and his eyelids dropped. A sweet fatigue spread over his limbs. He did not trouble to open his eyes even when he sensed Abla's children standing in the doorway. Now he heard their hesitant voices.

"The guest is sleeping," said the little girl.

"He's from Israel," said the boy.

"A Jew . . . "

"Shhh!" Her brother, alarmed, silenced her, as if fearing that she might stir up a force that no one could control.

"Does he have a gun?"

Her brother thought silently for a long time. "He's got one, but he keeps it where you can't see it."

"Where's Mommy?"

"She went upstairs," her brother answered. "She went upstairs after lunch."

"I didn't see her."

"Daddy went upstairs, too," he added.

"Why?"

"What do you mean, why?"

"Why did Mommy and Daddy go upstairs?"

"Dope!" Her brother, triumphant and superior, sneered at her. "I told you last week."

"What did you tell me?"

"He screws her. Every day he screws her and afterwards he lies on his back."

"I don't like to lie on my back," the girl said.

The two of them took their leave. The breeze through the window had died and the bird on the pomegranate tree had fallen silent. The poet's smile faded away, and his face flushed as if someone had slapped him. The couple making love upstairs were like a weight on his shoulders.

He begrudged Abla her pleasure. Characteristically, he sought consolation in words. She's got a squashed-in nose, he said to himself. It spread out over her mustache and her ratty teeth. Her hair is bristly. Her eyes may be clear, but they're small. Her ears— they're like a couple of torn rags. She probably gives off a bad smell from her mouth when she gets excited.

It angered him that he had had to defend himself against her. She had sat there on the other side of the table, tearing at her food like a rat, spanking him as if he were a naughty schoolboy. Wrathfully, he got up and left the room, found the bathroom, rinsed his face. He made his way out of the house muttering, "Let them go to hell! All of them!"

"All of them" meant the Israeli troops, the Arab spies, the couple making love upstairs, and even the bird singing on the pomegranate tree. The poet crossed the road and walked along the main street. He found a coffeehouse drowsing under the eucalyptus trees and sat down on a wicker stool. Behind his back, the soft click of the backgammon dice abruptly ceased. An aged shopkeeper in billowing black trousers was leaning against a tree trunk. He gaped at the poet with extreme wariness, as if he were a lizard. On account of Ramadan, the coffeehouse was nearly deserted, and the few customers were not offered drinks. One of the backgammon players said in a husky voice, "We thought we'd be spared their disgusting faces until Sunday."

Fatkhi gazed along the main street. There were no Jews there, neither soldiers nor civilians. The shopkeeper stooped in his filthy trousers and breathed heavily. Then he quickly straightened and examined Fatkhi with some trepidation, as if afraid that the poet had changed position. When he found everything as it had been, the old man cleared his throat and called, "Boy!"

An idiotic looking waiter, barefoot and gangly, came to him and said, "Eh?"

The old shopkeeper pointed at the ground under the poet's feet. "Go see what that crow wants here."

"Eh!" said the waiter.

Tiny hammers beat in Fatkhi's temples. The waiter hopped toward him, swinging his shoulders, and stopped two paces from his chair. Looking as if he were quite ready to run for his life, he shouted, "Eh?" Suddenly he bared his teeth and, smiling disparagingly at all the world's dangers, fired the provocative challenge, "Shalom!" in Hebrew, no less.

Fatkhi was not amused. He measured the "boy" who stood shifting his weight from foot to foot and said angrily, "Get lost."

His perfect Arabic pronunciation pleased the waiter but heightened the shopkeeper's suspicions. The backgammon players behind Fatkhi's back reacted as if some sacrilege had just been committed. The backgammon box was slammed shut in a small avalanche of wooden counters and dice. The husky voice murmured querulously in the clear air and an unctuous voice said, "Someday they'll start climbing to the top of the minaret on Fridays and preaching to us out of the Koran. Allah protect us from the devil!"

If Wasfy were here, the poet thought to himself, he'd know how to get out of this stupid fix. The poet had fled the dentist's house without his jacket and tie. His short-sleeved shirt was open down to the third button, and his pants indubitably carried an Israeli trademark. The idiotic waiter still stood there, grinning impudently. The poet lifted his arm in a sudden movement, as his mother used to when she shooed chickens from the courtyard. "Get going already! I told you to get out of here . . . "

Husky-voice came to life again. "Allah! Allah! He'll be shitting on your mat and giving orders inside your house soon."

"I'd like to screw him good," hissed the unctuous voice.

Where's Wasfy when I need him? Fatkhi thought, getting to his feet. He had to behave responsibly, accept the yoke of Party discipline. He mustn't provoke a disturbance in this town.

He rose, meaning to go. Even as he deliberately lit a forbidden cigarette, something to salvage whatever remained of his pride, he was thinking that it would be best to withdraw. He took two steps and the waiter retreated. But now the unctuous voice stung him in the ear: *"Tuz!"*—a contemptuous challenge to which any self-respecting man must respond.

The poet burned with an all-consuming flame. The image came to him of Fakhri carrying a Kalatchnikov machine gun on his shoulder and a pen in his right hand. Fakhri, who permitted himself to call the poet an "intellectual whore." Legs trembling with anger, Fatkhi approached a young man with long sideburns, whom he believed owned that unctuous voice that had whipped him and burned him with *"Tuz."* "You're a creature that stumbles in the darkness," the poet mocked him in flowery Arabic.

The young man was startled. "What does he want from me?" he asked his friends. His was actually the husky voice.

Fatkhi threw caution to the winds. "I'm an Arab, the son of Arabs, from Beit Netufa!" he proclaimed. He wanted to say that he was a refugee driven out of Mazraya, but he couldn't take back what he'd already said.

A lean young man with wicked eyes got to his feet and said in his unctuous voice, "And what brings you here, *Ya baba?*"

Again, *"Ya baba."* Back in the refugee camp he could not respond to the woman's scorn. Here, with the young man's mug before him, he answered harshly enough to put him in his place: "That's none of your business."

They were too close to one another. A sickly-looking man sitting some distance away intervened. "Let him go, boys. He's obviously come looking for a woman."

The young man backed off to his stool and spat out, "I guess they're human too!"

But the husky voice flared. "That's what really gets me. The Jews piss a whole shower of money down on them and then they come barging over here to buy our girls and daughters. I tell you, in another year or two, all we'll have left to fool around with will be she-donkeys."

The unctuous-voiced young man bleated with laughter. "Go to Nablus, kid," he said to the other man. "The Turks grabbed even your grandfather's she-donkeys—so why shouldn't the Jews do the same to yours?"

"You think that's a joke, eh?" the husky voice growled.

In his left ear Fatkhi heard another "Eh!" The young waiter touched his shoulder and held out a cup of filthy tea. Fatkhi ignored the idiot and ran off to the main street.

Entering the dentist's home, he was enveloped by silence but found no rest. From one of the other rooms there came the children's light voices and the maid's soft laughter. Abla was sitting in the armchair next to the bookshelf, working industriously on her students' notebooks. When he came in she hurriedly removed the reading glasses that gave her homely face an owlish expression, and asked in a velvet voice, "Don't you nap in the afternoon?"

You can hear the satisfaction in her voice, thought the poet. Her movements were less abrupt, her eyes clearer. Fatkhi knew these signs well. Although certain that he was not jealous, he was tempted to annoy this female taking her ease in the armchair. "I took a walk outside," he said.

"This place is too small," she said good-humoredly. "Everybody knows everybody else."

"I was sitting in a coffeehouse and I almost got into a fight." He felt a strong desire to shatter her composure.

"You can't cope with our young men." She laughed a short, feminine laugh and added: "You won't find a single gentleman among them. When they need to, they can really sink their teeth in."

"They were convinced that I was a Jew."

"I'll bet they saw you come into the house," she said with equanimity. "That should calm them down."

The poet gave up. "I'll go and take a nap."

The teacher let her maternal generosity flow over him. "You're tense, Fatkhi. The room upstairs on the left is prepared for you."

As he climbed the stairs her gentle voice called out, "Zuheir's coming tonight."

(1977)

—Translated by Edward Grossman

Sleepwalkers

⸌

JACOB BUCHAN

Once upon a time there were two men. About thirty-five years old. One was very rich. Their acquaintance began in summer and lasted only a few days. The rich man's name was Asaf Green.

This is how they met. In a small forest in the Galilee, north of the city of Sefad, Asaf, his wife, and their children set up camp from which they planned to take day trips in the area for about a week. Asaf owned a large printing plant in Haifa. He was short-tempered, sharp-tongued, impatient. Enjoyed life's pleasures, loved his wife, crazy about his kids; a world-class worrier. Woke up every morning with the feeling that today was the day of the catastrophe that would bring him to wrack and ruin.

In the fifteen years of his marriage he had never had another woman, no little affair on the side, no one-night stand. Day after day he came home from work, put everything and everybody in their place, demanded silence, showered, ate, fell into bed and onto his wife. Asaf was a dark, attractive man. The set of his mouth suggested both derision and shyness; his small, black eyes had an insolent expression. Curly hair, a heavy beard, a booming voice. His walk made him look as if he were moving sideways (if such a thing is possible), not forward.

A Border Patrol jeep pulled to a stop at a high clearing in the woods. An officer stepped out, gun in hand, and walked towards the large tent they had set up. Asaf went to meet him. The officer asked, "How many are you?"

"Five."

"Weapons?"

"Uzi."

"Do you know you're alone in the woods?"

147

His wife joined them. "Yes, that's what we wanted."

"Where are you from?"

"Haifa," said Asaf. "Where are you from?"

"That's no concern of yours. I protect you, you don't protect me."

"Listen to this guy! I'm only asking where you come from! You don't wanna tell us, so don't." He turned angrily to his wife and said, "Come on, let's go." After saying thank you to the officer, she too turned away.

"Take care," the officer said, and went on his way.

Late at night, the children were already asleep. Asaf and his wife were grilling meat, sitting around the fire drinking coffee from the pot they had put on the glowing coals. Asaf stirred it occasionally. The sound of a jeep approaching, the glow of its lights. The officer arrived. Asaf invited him to eat and drink with them. You call that meat, the officer jibed, but sat down to join them. Asaf handed him a mug of steaming coffee and asked, "Are you out looking for love nests, or what?"

The officer asked, "Aren't you afraid to be here alone in the dark?"

"No. What about you?"

"How old are you," the woman asked.

"Old enough."

"Married?"

"Oh boy," Asaf broke in, "in a minute you'll wanna know how many times a day he screws!"

"Your husband is the jealous type." The officer sat, legs crossed under him, his gun on his shoulder, sipping his coffee. His movements seemed deceptively graceful in the dimness. They stared at the coals, as if they wanted to absorb the remaining light. The officer took out a box of matches and lit one. He stared at the flame until it went out, then lit another one. The darkness of depression showed on his face, but they didn't see it. Asaf asked, "Don't you have anything better to do with yourself than wander around like this day and night?"

"No, I don't," said the officer staring at Asaf until he averted his eyes.

"Can you live on what you make?"

"I can live on less."

"How do you spend your time?" Asaf chewed a piece of meat.

"Wander around."

"That's a life?"

"In this line of work, there's plenty of time to think."

"What do you think about?" Asaf asked.

"About death," the officer answered in a hushed voice. He put his mug down, thanked them for the coffee, got up, and walked to the clearing amidst the trees. They didn't watch him. They sat in silence for a while.

"Can you beat that guy!" said Asaf, "Thinks about death!"

Osnat, his wife, said to him, "I want you to make sure the tent is sealed tight tonight."

"What's the matter?"

"I don't know. But I want you to do it."

They got up. Asaf urinated on the glowing coals which emitted a gust of smoke and then died out. They disappeared into the tent and closed it. Under the blanket, he cuddled up to his wife, whispering "So, you got an itch for me?"

" . . . yes."

Outside, beyond the canvas tent, a figure appeared and, with the stealth and agility of an animal, turned and moved swiftly away, the wind at its back.

Osnat was the first to wake up in the morning. The children were sleeping. Asaf was snoring lightly. She stretched and wrapped herself around him, mumbled something, closed her eyes. The remnants of a dream upset her. She couldn't remember. The atmosphere was so palpable. The intense light. What was in that dream? She got up wearily, noiselessly. She put on her pants, a bra, and shirt; she opened the tent and disappeared slowly outside. There she stood rooted to the spot.

Her eyes widened. Covered in goose flesh, she put her hand over her mouth to stifle a scream. She stepped backwards in terror, her back to the tent. She banged up against it, bent and hurled herself inside. She fell over Asaf's legs, and he stirred, mumbling, "What happened?" She shook him, speechless, eyes gigantic, pointing to the opening. He saw her and came instantly awake. "What happened, Osnat?!"

"There were people here during the night! They did things outside! Horrible things! Let's take the kids and get out of here right away, right now!"

Asaf took his gun, and still in his underwear, crawled quickly through the opening. Hanging on the trees around the tent were five cardboard death heads. The sight of them was so extraordinary and terrifying, so alien in the peaceful dawn of the woods. White light between the tree trunks, a thin mist hovering above the distant groves below. On the horizon, blue mountains like cats in a fog. Pine needles, remains of the campfire, the coffee pot, the mugs strewn about. He saw it all in a glance, and again he looked at the heads. They hung on the trees closest to the tent. Chills ran through him, "Ossie! Put the kids in the car!"

The sleepy children were dragged to the car, their whining an accompaniment to the shouts of Osnat and Asaf. She carried the baby in her arms. Asaf guarded them with his gun.

Five minutes later, Osnat yelled, "Where are you driving to?"

"To the police, stupid! The police! The army! This place is full of terrorists! I'll break that shmuck's head, the one from the Border Patrol! Protecting us! I can't believe they didn't just slaughter us!" While their car barreled down the winding road as if floodwaters were threatening to engulf them from behind, the Border Patrol jeep appeared from the opposite direction, bouncing along the road like a jumping bean. Asaf flashed his lights. They came to a stop, windows parallel. The night officer asked what happened. "You think everybody's looking for death like you, you son-of-a-bitch! Where's your protection! The woods are full of terrorists! Death heads!"

"Don't curse. I didn't curse either. I was on my way to see how you were. You gave me the impression that you didn't need me."

"You would have found us slaughtered! Give me your name and badge number!"

"Inspector Isam Medan, Neve Yosha Police," the Bedouin said.

Then he turned to Osnat—perhaps without even wanting to, he noticed that she hadn't taken her eyes off him—and said matter-of-factly to her, "Yesterday you asked me if I'm married, and then you didn't give me a chance to answer you. The answer is no."

"Why do you bother to answer me today?" Osnat asked him, not without a trace of anger, "What would you have done if we hadn't met again?"

"I don't like to leave things unresolved. We would have met."

Osnat was silent. She felt a little afraid of Asaf, who cut off their words with his body and aggressively put the car into gear and took off. Isam watched them, thinking about the pulsing artery in Asaf's neck, about Osnat's face and eyes. He blinked his light eyes, ran his tongue over his lips. Then he turned, got into his jeep, and drove quickly away.

Asaf and Osnat drove to the Neve Yosha police station without exchanging a word. His lips were a thin line of bitter hatred. Osnat pacified and consoled, answering the children's occasional questions. One of them was still wrapped in a blanket, dozing.

"What are you thinking about?" Asaf spat out the question.

"I still can't calm down. My whole body is shaking." She was also thinking about Asaf's behavior, about the harsh, controlling aspects of his character, his impatience. She felt the gap between them widening. Tears filled her eyes. Asaf stopped the car on the side of the road, opened a map, and busied himself looking at it. Suddenly he noticed Osnat's eyes.

Command cars and jeeps were racing around in all directions outside the police station. Asaf parked and, in his side-to-side, rolling gait, walked into the building with Osnat and their children. He went up to the desk sergeant sitting behind the high counter and quickly told him his story. The sergeant, older and easy-going, listened without writing down a thing. Only at the end of Asaf's story did he indicate that Asaf should come behind the counter and approach him. Asaf did so, and was shocked to see a large package wrapped in a blanket tied at the corners. Under the knots he could see the tent and some of the equipment they had left behind in the woods.

"Yours?"

"Yes. Wait a minute. How did this get here? What's going on? Someone's playing games with us!"

"We do what has to be done." The sergeant drummed his sharpened pencil on the counter.

"Who brought the package, Isam?"

"I really don't know. Please just tell me what's inside and you can take it and go."

The desk sergeant filled out a form listing the items in the package and making a note of their address and the events of that night, and they signed it. Asaf gathered up his property, loaded it into the car and they drove off.

A few days later, in the late morning, Osnat was sitting in her house in Haifa eating a slice of toast and cheese and spreading another slice with apricot jam she had made herself. Her eyes looked off into the distance, down to the foot of the mountain, wandering over roofs, dipping into the ocean, scanning the coastline, the pale spot of Rosh Hanikra, the ships at anchor, the cranes, the docks, the racing boats, the fluctuating colors of the water, the waves of heat shimmering in the air—the doorbell rang.

She roused herself, thought for a moment, asked who's there, heard, "Surprise."

An unfamiliar voice. She went to get dressed. Opened the door. A Border Patrol soldier who was standing there asked, "Are you Osnat Green?"

"Yes. What happened?"

"Inspector Isam Medan is sitting in the jeep. Asks if he can come up."

"Who?"

"Inspector Isam. From the Neve Yosha Police."

All at once she remembered, amazed at the knots in her stomach. She said to him, "Yes. Of course. What's the matter, can't he come up here without sending you first?"

"Don't know, Ma'am." He turned and went.

Isam appeared. The sight of him made her tremble. He said hello and didn't look at her body and didn't shake her hand. "Is Asaf home?"

"You know he isn't."

"How should I know?"

"No, you don't know."

"How are you?"

"Okay." She wondered.

"I brought you something." He sat down and opened his bag. His dark-skinned arms, his fingers and their white nails fascinated her. How calmly and surely he handled the buckles of his bag. He removed a pair of binoculars. "Yours. I found them too. And I apologize—if you'd like . . . " and he took out the cardboard death heads.

"Tell me, are you a sadist?"

"Look Osnat, I only found the binoculars recently. I took down the death heads that first day. I don't know if I'm a sadist. I couldn't come sooner because I was busy with routine security. I came today because of something else altogether, and I thought that as long as I was coming, I'd bring you these things. But bringing them was not my main purpose. For that I need Asaf."

"Why didn't you come in the evening?" She looked directly into his eyes. He didn't answer and he wasn't embarrassed.

"Oh, I forgot to offer you something to drink. You know, if Asaf came in now and saw you with me, he would kill you. What would you like to drink."

"So maybe I should go. I'd like black coffee, no sugar. It's nice and cool here. Maybe he'd kill you instead."

She got up gracefully and went into the kitchen.

The knitted fabric of her blouse was soft. It showed off her figure while leaving the lines of her body indistinct. It was comfortably smooth against her body. Caressing. Her legs were bare in cut-off jeans.

He got up and walked slowly to the kitchen. Leaning against the door frame, he watched her make the coffee. She hadn't heard him come, and suddenly seeing him there startled her so much that she spilled coffee on the floor as she was taking it off the gas. She cursed and bent to wipe it up.

"I didn't come in the evening because I wanted to see you alone. I think you have something to say to me."

She was suddenly frightened. The way he stood there. He blocked the whole kitchen. A man totally alien to her. Gun at his waist. His imposing height. That special smell of his. Her excitement. His eyes and mouth, his fingers. And his composure. What could possibly shake that composure? Me? Why me? She couldn't look directly at him.

"What are you talking about?" She poured a cup and held it out to him. He took it from her hand and she recoiled from any contact with his fingers, as if she were peeling cactus fruit. If only he would smile—then I would know there was no danger, that it's only a game.

"I'm talking about the fact that you're scared of me, the way you looked at me near the campfire and then again on the road. A look that comes straight from the heart before words can be formed."

"What do you want?" Osnat asked shifting her weight to one leg.

"To know. You see, if I know, then it will be easier for me to die when the time comes."

Osnat moved slowly towards the wall, looking out of the kitchen window at the distant ocean, the endless, frightening space, the light glittering on the water, the flickering reflections of lime-washed roofs.

"I'll tell you," she said in a hushed voice without turning her head. One of her eyes was slightly closed. Her lips were swollen.

"Asaf and I have a lot of money. He makes a fortune. I can do almost anything I want with money, get whatever my heart desires. Asaf wanted to come to live in Haifa, close to his plant. We moved here, but we have a house in Kiriyat Bialik, close to the open fields on the outskirts of town, close to tall trees, silk oak, jacaranda, pine, with a wide dirt road and oleaster hedges covered with honeysuckle and jasmine vines. There's a shaded front yard and a piece of land out back behind the house. We didn't rent it out. I refused. Sometimes my brother lives there, sometimes my sister and her children. Mostly, the house stands empty for months at a time, dusty, deserted, abandoned. Asaf pays monthly for security guards. It's the house that my mother left us, and Asaf bought out my brother and sister.

"Sometimes I drive out there, and in an attack of housecleaning fever, I air out everything, bring a water hose into the house and wash and scrub it all. I can't manage the garden. Then I sit down on the breezy patio where spots of light and shadow mark the wall and the floor tiles and my body, and I gaze at the fern tree, the avocado, the pecan, gaze and dream. Gaze and fantasize. Isn't it strange how things change, how the branches bend towards the ground from the weight of their fruit and their years. And I think about how I don't want even one inch of this house changed. No walls broken, no rooms added. This is how it has always been. Even twenty years ago the distance between the tree and the place I love to sit in was the same, exactly the same, as it is today. And here, sitting in this exact, almost private spot in the space between me and the tree, I know that this is where I belong, that this place belongs to me and I belong to it, to this land. I did my growing up in that space, which was large enough to encompass all those moments of sadness and joy, of contentment and suffering—everything. I know how the colors of these leaves change with the changing seasons, and how the air is sometimes permeated with the smell of fire. And sometimes there are the blossoms of the mandarin orange trees and birds that come to winter here, the cooing and the gurgling of the pigeons on the roof. No new house or landscape, no new furniture or rugs could ever replace this house, the land, the tree. This is the taste, the smell, the special light that is sometimes revealed to me that I love to see, almost to inhale it from a certain position, a specific angle. I feel it in my mouth, on my palate. Something sweet and full of grace like a prayer that has been answered. It is the deepest contentment I have ever known, maybe like the feeling a baby has when it is held in its mother's arms.

"Yes, so now I wanted to wreak a little havoc, destroy a little, put things out of joint. But—Asaf is that house, that piece of land. He is the trees. Too bad you asked questions. You look like a volcano. I waited for a gorgeous rainbow to emerge from your mouth, but only lava flowed out."

Isam looked at her over the rim of the cup, and only then did she turn her head towards him. Slightly embarrassed, blushing.

He smiled. A terrible smile. His gums were red, his teeth white. His eyes were all slits and wrinkles. He looked like a devil. Osnat said, "You weren't even listening to me. You didn't even hear, didn't understand."

"I understood, Osnat. We all want to keep what we have, and we want more. Always more. Something we can't reach."

Isam stayed where he was. He blocked the door of the kitchen with his size, his jumpiness, his tension. The only thing that filled her mind was how to get out of there without asking him to move out of the doorway, and what to do if he didn't move, and what if Asaf came in or called. Facing him, she became unnerved and she could feel fear spreading through her, winding endlessly through her body.

"Isam, I want to pass, I have to go. You can come in the evening. Asaf will be here."

He took a sip of coffee, looked at her, rolled the liquid around in his mouth and swallowed. Then he turned and walked through the living room to the door, opened it, and went out without saying a word. On the table were the binoculars and the death heads.

Isam returned late that evening. Asaf opened the door for him and said, "What's happening, pal? Are you the one who plays night games with us with masks?"

"I came to invite you to hunt wild pigs with me. I don't play night games."

"Come on in."

Asaf has already showered, is wearing shorts and an undershirt, his potbelly protruding. He fills the room with his shiny black beard and his imperious manner.

"Sit here!" He pounded on the back of a big, soft armchair. Isam sat down.

"You didn't come here to see little old me for just no reason at all. You want to compete with me for something. Beat me at something. Probably want to get at Osnat through me. A Bedouin coming to visit a married woman when her husband isn't home! Uh-uh, it's not right, not fitting, it just isn't done. What's really going on, you want to kill me!?"

Isam averted his gaze. The whites of his eyes reddened, his mouth set in disgust. He had the look of a person who cannot believe he is actually taking part in such a conversation.

"Osnat isn't here," Asaf fueled Isam's anger.

Isam was silent. Asaf continued, "Why all of a sudden do you want to hunt with me? When do you want to go?"

"Friday evening. Come Thursday night. Sleep at my place in Rosh Pina. Friday we'll stake out the territory. We'll hunt at night. On Saturday you can bring your wife enough meat for six months."

"Why me?" Asaf insisted.

"Because of your disease," Isam answered quietly and looked into Asaf's face, into his eyes. He was rotating his wrist round and round.

"Disease?"

"The disease of jealousy."

"What happened to you?" asked Asaf, changing the subject, moving his chin in the direction of Isam's hand.

"Well, you certainly are perceptive, you notice everything. That's good and not so good when you hunt. I got caught in a skirmish between Jews and Arabs under Nisnas Bridge. A fight about the right to throw junk into the auto graveyard."

Asaf looked at him, nodded his head, and said, "Tell me, doesn't it seem strange to you, the way you're pursuing us? Taking an interest in us, taking the trouble to return our property, asking how we feel, visiting my wife, inviting me to hunt—doesn't it seem just a little peculiar to you?"

Isam gave a little smile and immediately concealed it. "No. It seems peculiar to me that you feel the need to ask me. Ask yourself why the questions. Ask yourself why you can't see these things in a positive light, why you can't take my invitation as a friendly gesture towards you. In any case," here Isam's words became harsher, "I'm going now. I live in Rosh Pina, near the wellspring overlooking the cemetery in the wadi below. Ask anybody. I'll wait for you until ten in the morning. You don't have to bring anything with you. Only yourself." He got up and went. Asaf stood blinking and, pursing his lips, let out a snorting laugh and then another one. "Black son-of-a-bitch."

The new orange Volkswagen van climbed the steep, slippery, stone-paved road to the western part of Rosh Pina. Osnat had urged him to go. Forced him to, really. "So you won't be home for a night or two. So what? Go. I'm interested to know what happens between the two of you."

"You think I'm going to fight for you, right?"

"Of course."

"Whore! Women are such whores!"

"As if men aren't. He came right into our home, I still can't figure out why he didn't rape me . . . he was really dying to."

The van bounced on the smooth stones . . . bounced . . . And Asaf yearned to bash Isam's skull to pieces.

A man sat on the wooden steps of his house cleaning a rifle. A double-barreled rifle was lying beside him, another was propped up against the banister. Shiny, with a carved, dark wooden stock, its barrel thick and black. The silver bolt was also covered with engravings. The magazines were unusual. It was seven in the morning. Isam didn't seem surprised, only his eyes glowed. Smiling, he invited Asaf to sit. Asaf remained standing. Isam finished cleaning the rifle, "This is a Krupp!" He tossed it to Asaf, who caught and examined it. "I inherited it from my grandfather who was a member of the Jeorana tribe of the Hula area. Some Russian settler from Yesod Hamala gave it to him as a gift at the end of the last century. Double trigger, twelve-millimeter cartridges. A range of fifteen to twenty meters. It can put a hole in your lungs the size of a soccer ball."

"Can I call Osnat?"

"Sure, go right on in. The telephone is in the kitchen."

Asaf crossed the tree-shaded patio and entered the house. There were only pillows, mats, and carpets on the floor, and large clay and copper vases. Stuffed and mounted animal heads. Antlers. Bedouin drums. All kinds of knives. A beaded curtain. Crossed rifles. Asaf was dizzy from the intensity of color that filled the large room, which had no television or radio or books in it. He bent his head to pass through the low doorway into the kitchen. One entire wall was a window that looked out onto the wadi, and the intense shade of green that filled the room through it was blinding. There was an enormous refrigerator and a set of knives and saws.

Asaf called Osnat and when she asked to talk to Isam he got upset and began to question her. She got angry, and he cursed her and slammed down the phone, thinking that he was bringing disaster down on himself and his family.

Isam came in to call him. He looked at him and then went and opened the freezer. A tremendous amount of frozen meat was packed inside. Isam said, "I'll explain. I do it all. From the beginning. I stake out the territory. Set up the ambush. Stalk. Hunt Transport. I saw the leg joints, remove the hair, carve, clean, cure. And here—"

"Do you have a wife? Who do you do all of this for?" Asaf asked in surprise.

"In a minute you'll want to know how many times a day I screw. It's for me. I am a predator."

They drove to the Hula Reserve in Isam's jeep to stake out the territory and set up the ambush. When they arrived, Isam drove through a yellow field to the shade of a eucalyptus grove bordered by tall, tangled raspberry thickets. He jumped out of the jeep and asked Asaf offhandedly, "Are you having a problem?" Asaf, red-eyed, glanced at him, shaking his head no, and said immediately, "You probably screw all the girl soldiers in your unit." Isam stopped what he was doing and turned toward him, "Not even one."

"So it probably has calluses on it from so much rubbing . . . "
Isam narrowed his light eyes and in a flash, he opened his pants
and removed them—he had no underwear on—held his large,
smooth, brown penis in his hand and showed it to Asaf. Asaf
gulped in confusion, but managed to say, "You probably want me
to turn around . . . "

Isam zipped up his pants quickly, signaling to Asaf with his
head to join him. Isam shouldered his rifle, put his pack on his
back, gave Asaf a large jerrycan of water strapped into a carrier. A
hunting knife banged against his thigh. They walked. Asaf became
excited by the thought of Osnat seeing Isam's penis. He followed
Isam, eyes glazed.

Isam turned to Asaf and explained, "The wild ducks I used to
hunt here in the early evening always flew in pairs. I would hit one
and after a while, its mate would return. I've hunted pelicans,
martens, porcupines, egrets here."

Asaf walked along beside him. He was wound up and tense.
He didn't feel like doing anything. He wanted to ask Isam once
and for all about that night in the woods, what the investigation
had turned up about the cardboard death heads—but he didn't.
He'd always believed that a strong person was someone who could
stick to his decisions, even if he wasn't satisfied with them. And he
wasn't used to dragging along after someone without knowing
what was in store, without having had the experience before. From
that point on, Asaf continued to walk and listen, but he didn't
hear.

Isam talked about the low, bright, purplish Naftali Mountains
to the east. He described the basalt crust that covered the area,
and the alluvial fans that created the Kishon and Hazor Rivers. He
explained how Hula nettles cured stomachaches.

Isam, in a kind of ecstatic trance, said to Asaf, "When I walk
here, it is as if I am walking inside my own soul. Everything is so
beautiful, so complex, everything is basalt." They walked past
small lakes, shallow ponds, on which the pure white petals of
water lilies floated alongside the thick foliage of bulrushes and
cattails. A flock of birds, terns, skimmed across the surface of the
water, then billowed up and flew off. Now and then, the strong
smell of silt permeated the air, along with the scent of the open
fields.

They came to the end of the windy, shaded area and Isam
halted. He removed his backpack, telling Asaf to take off the water
carrier. He gathered and made a pile of several rocks, quickly lit a
fire on which he placed the pot he had removed from his pack.

He added some sage leaves from a jar, took out a large pita bread, yogurt, some olives from a jar, and some herbs. Leaning up against the tree trunks, they ate. Asaf's eyes filled with tears from the intensity of pure, simple pleasure, from the sense of harmony and oneness he felt with the surroundings. They sat in silence for a while. Isam prepared tea, saying suddenly, "This place is much more sharply defined than a printing plant. This is where the fine line between life and death is, a place with its own hidden laws! Who, or maybe what, causes me to stalk the pig? What causes the pig to survive? Who is responsible for this special relationship between us? In this place, everything I am and everything I know is gathered together and compressed for a brief moment.

He gulps tea noisily from his mug. His arm is thin, strong and sinewy, his fingers long and dark. Asaf looks at them, imagining them pressing a rifle trigger, fondling a woman's buttocks. Carving up raw, writhing flesh. Isam continued. "At night, I cover myself with mud—you'll cover yourself with ointment against mosquitoes, and a lot of it. And not just once. My blood is too thick for a mosquito to suck. For years I trained myself not to hear their buzzing. I want to eliminate the smell of my blood so the wind can't carry it to the nostrils of the pig. I mash swamp clover leaves and mix them with the mud I rub over my body. What I try to do is lead the pig into the barrel of my rifle. I track it during the day, as you will soon see, locate some of its trails and leave socks that I have worn for a while and a sweaty shirt strewn along them. Taking into consideration wind direction, which I know how to identify from experience, I lead it to a trail where there are supposedly no humans, and there I sit in wait for it. Only the eyeteeth of a wild pig can cut through the thick foliage, cattails, and bulrushes strong as metal bars, so it leaves a trail when it passes through to drink."

His light eyes open wide, Isam continued. "Once I was sitting with friends near some ponds in the shrubbery not far from the coast. I was lying in wait for some land ducks or egrets. But they didn't come anywhere near us, as if something had warned them of danger. Slowly I began to understand: I was the one warning them. I was transmitting to them my tension, my pangs of conscience, my murderous intentions, my fears. Try it sometime: get out of your car where you see pigeons perched on electric power lines. They won't move. Aim your slingshot at them, just aim it, and they instantly fly away. I would take a book or newspaper with me, sit in the bushes, and forget about them. They would approach, come right up to me, and I would pick them off one by one with no trouble at all. My friends would say things like, so you found a good spot, that's all. I would laugh, and switch places with them. And of course, the same thing happened again. I am completely unaware of myself when I shoot them. If I weren't, they would become aware of me first. You have to feel that you are right on the edge of disaster, you almost have to stop being. You have to relinquish the 'I' and become something else. A pig, for example. And I'm amazed, because you see, that's really what people do all the time—even you, Asaf. You didn't come here to hunt with me, you came to put your wife, Osnat, to the test."

Isam got up quickly, spilled out the remains of his tea without looking at Asaf, who didn't drink, scattered the coals and stones and covered them with leaves. Then he put on his backpack and, hands on hips, stood looking at Asaf. Pointing to his head, Asaf said, "You're a sick man. What is it with you?" Isam stared at him, smiled, and turned away.

They returned to Isam's house in the hot afternoon wind, after Asaf had followed Isam tracking wild pigs through narrow, dangerous, and menacing paths of cattails from which there was no turning back. Their rifles had been cocked, magazines full. They left their odorous traps and Isam chose a spot for Asaf and one for himself, marking them with small pieces of white ribbon so they could find them at night.

Back in his house, Isam told Asaf, "Now you should go to sleep. I'll prepare things and then wake you. That's what I think we should do. But we could also grill some meat and drink wine, then later . . . "

A stone house in Rosh Pina shaded by a giant mulberry tree, overlooking the wellspring near the synagogue. A cold house, a clean one. Its window frames painted turquoise, its walls a pure, shining white. Spider webs in the corners like old lace curtains. And silence, such silence! A flowing silence, as bright as milky white light. A soft silence that comforts the heart, soothes the eyes, heals the skin and muscles, broken only by the sleepy, whistling wind from the wadi.

Night. Isam organized everything, checked the rifles, packed the binoculars, the mosquito ointment for Asaf, knives, first-aid kit, flashlights, matches, flare gun, water, towels, rope, small mats, "and a lot of patience," he added. They decided that they would signal each other by whistling.

They drove for almost an hour before Isam parked the jeep. He moved silently among the thickets as easily as if it were broad daylight. Everything was pressed up flat against his body, his dark clothes. In the moonlight, moving wordlessly through the maze of shrubbery and strange whistling sounds, gliding through the water, he brought Asaf to the place of the ambush. Although Asaf moved heavily, he wasn't gawkish. It seemed to him that Isam was trying to hide a smile at his awkwardness. In his own language, almost soundlessly, Isam whispered "good luck." He turned and disappeared with the agility of a deer.

Asaf sat down on the mat, laid his rifle across his knees, removed his binoculars and his canteen. He sighed involuntarily. "Moron! How did you wind up in such a situation! Like a heavy, tired, thirty-five-year-old water buffalo come to its final resting place in the bushes. In a little while a snorting pig will sniff you out. Of course, it won't know that you're not a water buffalo. It'll sink its yellow teeth into you and devour your liver; it'll crush your spine, scrape its smelly whiskers all over you, Osnat's husband, all over his sensitive red skin, his pampered potbelly, his troubled brain. What prompted you to abandon your own soul for hers, to take part in such an escapade? This is not you. It doesn't suit you. You who run the gamut from feeling totally in control, all-knowing, and solid to feeling an ugly sense of inferiority. There is a kind of basic emotional poverty about you, dark, weak, and perverse, which causes you to confuse things. Isam doesn't know, he still doesn't understand that he is a psychopath who could kill me without blinking an eye, that he lives in a world in which everything is clear and defined, and he has no need for questions. There isn't an ounce of curiosity in him. He feeds on the needs of his inferiors whom he controls through his rank, ability, or personality, or through that mysterious quality of his. Sure he's a good hunter. Why shouldn't he be? No guilt. No punishment. No nerves or feelings. War. He doesn't need anyone. Only himself. There is nothing growing within him, no fields to be plowed, planted, and harvested. He has only cold truth. Only judgments. Nothing human. And he can't form close relationships. I don't want him, don't want to be like him. Why am I attracted to him?!"

The moon inundated the shrubbery and the dark stone path with a kind of magic, hypnotic light, creating strange, frightening shadows. Everything was silvery, silvery green, silvery black, silvery yellow. Quivering plants floated on silver ripples of polluted water, a giant swamp turtle turned over—the sounds of his body dissolved into the silence of the forest. "I would be desolate without her. I feel ruined beyond repair. I haven't hummed a tune for months. And now the humming of mosquitoes. Indefatigable, circling around my head, near my neck, inside my clothes. In this light which is neither light nor darkness, like a coma, the sleep that is neither death nor wakefulness. How the feeling of my love for Osnat creeps upon me and fills my being, and I can live only if my love is accepted. Not me. My love. Put everything to the test. Every day and all day, if you get everything you want, minute after minute, then it's all right. If not, you destroy the whole works. You're a coward too, because you have no real strength, only tricks, only smart moves. Never satisfied. You don't have patience for anything. Everything has to be for your pleasure, for your immediate gratification which is always fleeting, wasted. You always have to pay the price. It's hard for you to express intimacy and easier for you to destroy than to build. Destruction suits you, because it's irresponsible and attracts a lot of attention. Destruction is constant tension. Always waiting for the next time you can be so highly charged up that you can forget the pain of the time before. Always the feeling of having missed something, maybe in another place, maybe with someone else. Perhaps once, only once, I will be able to achieve real peace of mind.

"What is all of this pondering, this weeping, this heartache, these small pleasures . . . understanding isn't life, and life doesn't change through understanding. Once my father told me (the Nazis furrowed his back with whips as they marched him to the ovens) that happiness can be found anywhere . . . And a girl who once loved me said that even a passing moment can be lifetime . . . "

Asaf was no longer sure of what he saw. Frightening silence. Everything was blurred by fog and mist. Pigs throwing smoke bombs? A fiery cat wearing blazing underwear in hell? He whistled. The sound dissolved in the dampness, unanswered. He was already lying on his side, his rifle on his thighs. He propped up his head with the palm of his hand against his cheek. His eyes closed, opened. Heavy. His hair silvery curls. Moonlight penetrated his eyes, his throat, his sweet thoughts. Such weariness. Asaf drifts off.

Five shots sliced through his sleep.

(1989)

—Translated by Sondra Silverston

Excerpt from
The Night of the Kid

⌁

Shin Shifra

A Chapter from the Novella

Afeefa* tucks the white breast into her embroidered bodice.
Are her eyes moist? She bundles the baby in the blanket and
puts him back in the hollow of the orange-tree basin, then returns
to the tub of the boiled wash. The washing twists quickly between
her hands, like water snakes. "The second wash is always shorter,"
mother explains. But to me it seems that Afeefa's brisk movements
hold back the cataract of tears which threatens to burst from her
throat. She must not. Afeefa hides her tears not only from the girl
watching her from the raised bank of earth. Must not court evil.
It seems to her that she has felt with her finger a first front tooth.
She hopes to live to fling it high against the sun when it falls out.
Take this donkey's tooth, she would say, and give me a doe's tooth
in its place, to calm the child's fear when he feels the sudden gap
in his mouth.

The swollen painful breast draws her glance back to the baby.
The girl will tell her father, the *moualem*.† And then perhaps the secret would slip out of her mouth. The baby's singed foot. Mother
is afraid to propose a doctor. "What if, God forbid," she dare not
utter the words. Let them consult the doctor, Afeefa allows herself
to dream, her hands lingering on a white slipcover. Perhaps in her
heart of hearts she wishes the *moualem* would offer to help. But
she did not untie the diapers before them. How can she reveal the
burn. "He's somewhat small, somewhat weak, it's cool under the
tree, he might catch cold, God forbid," she apologizes to the

---

*Afeefa: An Arabic woman's name, meaning "The Pure One."
†Moualem: Arabic, "teacher."

moualem's wife who suggests taking the baby's blanket off. With her own eyes she has seen how all the *moualem*'s children fell ill with red blotches all over their bodies and even their faces. After a few days their flesh was again as it had been. How can she forgive her womb for failing to grow the baby properly. At the end of the hot season, in the middle of the month, before the moon was full, he took her to wife.

Father calls me to come to the table, opens his mouth wide with every spoonful. A Viennese soup, it is called. Special for wash-days and Fridays. Airy semolina dumplings and vegetables. "What vegetables didn't I put in the pot, and still you don't eat," Mother scolds. When Afeefa is here I give up Father's stories and hurry back to the tree basin. But Father chooses to persist today. "My mother suckled me until I was three years old. Imagine. I used to bring over a small stool to sit at her knee, and I made the blessing." I can hardly swallow. But for Afeefa I'd have run to the end of the orange grove to throw up. "Enough, I can't eat any more." I slip away to the raised earth.

At the end of the hot season, surrounded to suffocation by women sprinkling rosewater and ululating hand on mouth, Afeefa came to the palace house. Outside a hot east wind was blowing. If only there were a scrap of cloud in the west to break the *hamsin*. If she were not a bride, surrounded by women. On the bank of the river she would harvest purplish sugar cane with a broad-bladed knife. In the faraway days boys used to sell them in the street of sand. She cuts the cane close to the joint between segments. The upper ones are sweeter. Places each piece on a rock and cleaves its rind with even strokes of the knife. Finally she splits them in four and puts them in her lap. Presses a piece to her lips, sucks its crystallizing sap, chews it between her teeth, her jaws set hard, sucking and sucking. The spray of the waterfall moistens her dry sources. Sometimes she sits on the dam in the waterfall, allowing the water to wet her gowns to the skin. As though she were a chimney for the *hamsin* wind. Again and again it enters at the upper gate with the grains of dust, passes through her innards, and exits through the body's lower gate. At any moment the blazing wind will burst from her mouth like a fire-spitting hyena and burn her body up. Her toes retain the memory of the kid's moist tongue. Since he has grown into a horned he-goat with a powerful rutting odor the neighbours bring their goats to the lean-to. But now, in the palace house, the scent of rosewater turns her stomach. If only there were a tiny cloud in the west. The rain would lay the *hamsin*, awaken the scent of the orange peel, and dispel the rose sweet-

ness. Ever since her father went to the land-of-no-return, ever
since the mill fell silent and the water flowed untamed, broke
down the dike, ever since the blood burst out of his veins, his
heart stopped—she is hired to work in the big packing-shed
around the palace house on the hilltop. That was what Afeefa in-
wardly called the house on the edge of the orange grove. Who
could have guessed that she would be its master's wife. Mounds of
oranges, brassy, glossy, press against the reed fence bounding the
packing shed on the east. Was it not on this side of it that I tried
in vain to pull a giant orange through a square in the lattice during one of our family excursions to "Seven Mills" to ask Afeefa to
come to a washday. "Jarisha is the name of the village," Father cor-
rects us. "And it isn't seven but eleven pairs of millstones." The
packaging paper has a sharp scent like the spikenard in summer.
Squatting among the packers, no one is so nimble as she at wrapping the fruit. Outside, hammers bang on the soft hoops binding
the wooden crates, white as the living skin. The man holds the
nails in his mouth, pushes them in one by one and hammers
round and round.

In the second year of the drought, if the rain does not fall
there will be no harvest. The packing shed will stand abandoned.
Windfall oranges will cover the ground and a sour fermenting
smell of rot will spread as far as the village houses. The barley
stubble has been cropped down to the ground. The herd of water
buffalo has abandoned the marshes and plodded over to the river-
bank. The waterfall tumbles over peacefully. Sometimes she wakes
up at night in alarm. The murmur of the waterfall, why cannot she
hear the murmur of the waterfall? An east wind shakes the eucalyptus trees on the banks of the river and the reeds rustle in re-
sponse. If only the rain would fall and wash the drooping palm
fronds in the village square. She will open her mouth to the large
drops, swill the water from cheek to cheek, rinse out the grains of
sand gritting between the teeth. There will be no harvest. The
water tanks have dried up. The wells are silent. Sand fills the water
channels in the orange grove. The leaves of the citrus trees have
turned yellow. During the heat they pumped water in hoses, even
with machines, from the river. But the water-greedy citrus did not
ripen. There will be no harvest. The village is shut up tight. No
more washdays at the *moualem*'s house. She need only cross the
wire fence and there she is on the street of sand.—It is forbidden,
says her mother, when they visit her father's grave in the hillside
cemetery during the summer. The hill is bare. Only some fleshy
agaves shelter the tombstones. The watchman for the Moslem

Council grows watermelons as far as the wire fence. Wild plants, what do they care for rain. In the hot days of that year their bellies were filled with watermelons. Watermelons and bread. Her mother told her, In the middle of the night three armed riders came knocking on the great wooden gate. Their faces wrapped in *keffiehs,* only their eyes showed. The master of the palace house opened to them and was forced to let the visitors into the courtyard. He alone and three rifle barrels. They did not return his greeting nor did they mince their words. Tomorrow. Fifty pounds Palestinian. They would come to collect in person. For the coffers of the revolt.* Has he not heard? Abd el-Kadr did not pay, they uprooted half his orange grove. A whole hectare.

In the second year of the drought, no sooner did the slim-wanded squills appear on Mount Napoleon, than the women went out at full moon to the stubble field north of the river. The dervish had read the omens. A haze covered the sun.—Tomorrow, tomorrow, he prophesied. But Afeefa knows. The time has not come. They will pray in vain. Her fingers come back dry.

Her mother pleads, They will say we are Egyptians, and Egyptians are godless. But the winding Yarkon is not the great river of Egypt. Daughter, we are fatherless, so speaks her mother about her father, as though she too were his child. Since the millstones came to a stop as did father—the vanes of the water wheel have broken. So she mourns him. An upper millstone, who would have thought it, of black basalt. Yet it is the way of the world that sandstone is the first to wear down. Mother does not refer by name to Calmaniyah bint Mohammed of Jamastin a-Sharqi, it is enough for her to say to Afeefa, They will say you are Egyptian. It was said that she went with a basket of eggs to the Jewish village. Did not even enter the main street. Sold to the housewives on the hill opposite. At night the men of the revolt burst into the tent. Strange that the dogs did not warn her. In her sleep. She left a year-old baby. Afeefa submits to her mother.

A large crowd has gathered in the stubble field. Beating tin oil-drums—Lord, give us rain, give us clouds. The sticks beating on the tins stop in midair. All eyes turn to them when they arrive. Afeefa lags behind. Children with swollen bellies make a circle around her—when? when? and this time the eyes look at her accusingly.

They waited for three days. A haze hung over the river in the morning, swathing the tops of the palm trees. On the fourth day the dervish saw omens—a southern, Egypt wind is blowing. Afeefa

*The reference is to the Palestinian Arab uprising of 1936–1939.

knows, the time has not come. The sky looks like tin. In the palm-
tree square the women alone gather. Only the virgins and moth-
ers. Each woman holding a black hen, plucking its feathers, Give
rain, give clouds. The squawking of the hens rose with the
women's prayers. Afeefa obliges her mother, carries a hand-mill.
She sits down in the middle of the square, on the tamped earth,
turning the upper millstone, empty, empty, the time has not come,
her hand waving away the black feathers flying in her face. The
women ululate hand on mouth.

In the third year the larder in her mother's house was empty.
Afeefa wanders as far as "Ten Mills" to gather nettles. She attempts
to grip the stem near the root. On her return she carries on her
head a bundle wrapped in a handkerchief, but her hands are
burning. Mother will boil the leaves and cook them as cutlets, No
worse than spinach, she claims. The villagers say that the men do
not even object to coots. They hold their noses and hasten to
bring them home. The women skin them quickly to discard the
reek and the children gladly bury the skins in the field and enjoy
the flesh of the coot in the evening. In the village it is said that
whoever eats the "Jews' dung"* will also stink in the end. And her
father says that in fact, the bird's vile smell comes from the plant
that it eats.—Should the sheep eat it, they too would smell vile.
Why, then, of all the plants of the field, has the coot chosen to eat
this plant? But two women alone, ever since her father went to the
land-of-no-return—who will catch coots for them. She wanders in
the stubble field, followed by the scrawny goat cropping every
scrap of grass. The goat is their assurance. Her mother will pour
the milk into a white cloth bag and hang it on a peg. It will drip all
night and by morning it will be a sourish *labaneh*.† Her mother has
already sold the Turkish *mejjideh* coin she used to wear around her
neck in order to buy barley. She sits on the mill, O Lord of the
World, what shall we eat? We have eaten the roots of the vetch. O
Lord of the World, why, what for? We have eaten the roots of the
wild artichoke. O Lord of the World, why do you hide your face?
she mumbles. And Afeefa pleaded for the life of the goat kid, with
its sprouting beard and soft horn-buds. Attached to her like a dog,
it follows her wherever she goes. Her mother says, It is somebody's
soul. It bleats to greet her return when she is still on the edge of
the village, just inside the cactus hedge.

---

*"Jews' Dung": A common Arabic name for an ill-smelling plant; *chara
fragils* in Latin.
†Labaneh: A thick yogurt made from goat's milk.

In the third year of the drought, at full moon, in the second
month of the rainy season, she sneaks into the scorched fields
which face the palace house on the edge of the orange grove.
Since her father died she has given up sleeping alone in the alcove. Her mother sleeps, her mouth open like a fish, beads of
sweat on her forehead. Today she has gone as far as "Ten Mills" to
gather nettles. The flame in her hands has already died down, but
her body feels scorched. Her skin wants to turn inside out. Four
times do silkworms shed their skins, and so does the snake. If this
were a proper season, the hill on her left would be clothed in
green down and the rosy stately squills would kindle the skyline—
When the squill blossoms, expect rain, her father used to foretell.
In vain did the fellahin turn up their fields. The clods are dry as
cattle droppings. Afeefa quits the encircling cactus fence, walks
past the abandoned mills. The palm trees sheltering their roofs
rustle their drooping fronds. The village sleeps. Even the hound
dogs are silent. The jackals have migrated to the hills. In vain does
the ear strain for the throbbing of the well, night's heartbeat. A
smell of burning hangs in the air, as though it were midsummer.
Only without the sharpness of the spikenard and the freshness of
dew. Her nostrils breathe a false wind and she turns her back to
the gate of the grove. Before her lies the open alfalfa field as far as
the stand of fragrant acacias on the east. The clods of scorched
earth hurt the soles of her feet and the dryness in her body urges
her to walk on and on. The kid follows in her footsteps.

She squats in the middle of the scorched field. Opposite is the
arched gate leading to the orange grove. The tendrils of the wild
rose have shriveled up. An avenue of palm trees leads from the
gate to the house which rises from the dark grove, surrounded by
a wall with a big square barred gate. A white dome overlooks flat
roofs bordered with a parapet, which gaze at the orange grove
through pottery pipes. What does the orange grove look like
through the eyes of those pipes? She lies on her back in the
ploughed field, her legs outstretched. The he-goat at her feet licks
her big left toe. It passes its tongue from toe to toe till it reaches
the little one, then passes to the big right toe. Afeefa uncovers her
smooth black hair to the moon. Don't know where I got this one
with her straight hair, her mother would say, amused, plaiting her
hair in those faraway days, when the vanes of the water wheel still
turned the millstones, and her father humped sacks of grain on
his back as though they were windborne tumbleweed. In front of
the mirror given her by the *moualem*'s wife, in the little alcove, she
combs her hair unseen. Now she loosens the two blue beads at the
end of the string braided into her plaits and lays them in the slack

of the skirt between her legs. She unlooses her braids, rises on her elbows, and looks at the house opposite, beyond the house, far away, there the sea lies. Would that a scrap of cloud rise in the west. Slowly slowly she lies back and rests her head on the earth. The kid licks her toes, sucks them one by one. Its soft teeth tickle. A moisture rises from the tips of her toes, climbs up her body. A hot east wind, blowing through me as through a chimney, get out of my body. Little cloud, rise from the west, glow above the dried vine arbor on the palace house roof, let lightning pierce the black orange grove, let thunder come to the silence, let moisture rise in my burrows. The white kid stands at her head, passes a rough tongue on her forehead, stops at her earlobes, sucks the tip of her nose, anoints her seared lips. She is stretched tight from her toes to the ends of the hair that crowns her head on the ground. Until a sea breeze burst through the lower gate. Her body like a bellows blew up a western wind. Lightning slashed the sky. A flock of clouds galloped to the east and swallowed up the moon. Large drops raised whirligigs of dust when they struck the scorched ground. The kid lapped her salty eyes and the source of joy—honey.

Did the man destined to be her son's father sit on the flat roof, shriveled vine tendrils fluttering over his head, gazing at the thirsty orange grove and beyond it to the east, to the expectant ploughed alfalfa fields, pleading and even demanding rain? From time to time he rises from his seat, turns to the parapet on the west side, searching for a little cloud from the sea. Alone. His sons, daughters-in-law, and grandchildren, even his old mother, always awake like a barn-owl—all sleep. Did he watch her from his post on the flat roof? Did the gleam of the goat kid in the moonlight give her away. Did his youth return and were his trousers moistened with forgotten pleasure. It is not right, not proper of me. One more year of drought and the orange grove will fall to the axe. That night he resolved to take Afeefa to wife.

Thirty days after he saw her from the roof, bringing the rain with her witchcraft, after his messengers went to carry his proposal to her widowed mother, and despite all his aged mother's warnings, A daughter of the Majanin* tribe. And why did the Abu Kishak clan† cast them out? Egyptians, mad folk, witchcraft. Have you not seen how the children run after her calling, When, when? meaning rain. And did they not tell that she befriends gypsies and the children of the shepherds. Her father's only child. Like father

---

*Majanin: Local Arabic name for a group of migrant tribes.
†The Abu Kishak clan was the principle clan on the banks of the Yarkon River.

like daughter. Green blood. And her father never took another
wife but her mother. He who loves a slave becomes his slave. And
they are slave folk. Thirty days after he saw her from the roof a
flood came down on the earth.

In the women's room, when her face was revealed to him, she
looked at him without lowering her eyes. Her painted lips parted,
come, man, come, they tempted him lustily. Did she wear that
night the gown Mother had given her, its neckline embroidered
with sequins, which an aunt had sent us from America? My
brother Nachman argued, "It's a waste. They sleep in their
clothes." "How do they have children then," I query. "You're too
little. You can't understand," he silences me. That night I
dreamed a spiral tower, twisting up to the sky beside the sea. I run,
I spin up the staircase. Behind me, a brown-skinned gypsy, like the
image of Hagar that used to hang in our living room after the
house on the land was sold and mother urged father to buy a sit-
ting-room suite, table, sofa, and two armchairs as well as a picture.
She wears a big nose-ring. There is a blue star tattoo in the center
of her forehead. She wears gown over gown, as we do for Purim
masquerade. Father takes black silk gowns from the wardrobe,
likewise preserved from the parcels of the aunt in America. "A
simple and impressive costume," he persuades the womenfolk.
One black gown and on top of it another black gown, whose skirts
he takes up to form a head-covering and a veil. "It doesn't look at
all like Afeefa," I grumble. "Like Arab townswomen," Father en-
treats, "in Jaffa, Jerusalem." But the gypsy woman in my dream
wears several gowns, all billowing as she runs after me. I run and
run up the spiral staircase, in diminishing, rising circles, and she
follows me in the darkness. The waves break against the tower wall
with the swirling of her gowns. I am near the top of the tower with
her after me. I feel her breath on the back of my neck. Then suddenly I am awakened by the terror and sweet pleasure awaiting me
at the top of the tower. But Mother gave Afeefa that gown years
before she was married. When she came to us, a girl, trilling softly,
*ya bint al sheikh al arab,** and moved like a dancer from the washtub
to the cauldron. We would wait for her on the big veranda, to see
her walking up the street of sand with her arms moving like wings.
Now, in the palace house, what use has she for mother's gift,
which must have become worn with the years.

(1990)

—*Translated by Yael Lotan*

*"O Daughter of the Sheikh of the [Bedouin] Tribe."

Cocked and Locked

ᔍ

ETGAR KERET

He's standing there in the middle of the alleyway, about twenty meters away from me, his *kaffiyeh* over his face, trying to provoke me to come closer: "Zbecial Force Cocksucker," he shouts at me in a heavy Arabic accent.

"What's up, *ya* Blatoon Hero? Your cross-eyed sergeant bush it up your ass too hard yesterday? Not strong enough to run?" He unzips his pants and takes out his dick: "What's up, Zbecial Force? My dick not good enough for you? It was blenty good for your sister, no? Blenty good for your mother, no? Blenty good for your friend Abutbul. How's he doing, Abutbul? Feeling better, boor guy? I saw they bring in a zbecial heligobter to take him away. Like a crazy-man he ran after me. Half a block he ran like a *majnun*. Blatsh!! His face squashed up like a watermelon."

I pull up my rifle till I have him dead center in my sights.

"Go ahead and shoot, *ya* Homo," he screams, unbuttoning his shirt and jeering. "Shoot right here." He points at his heart. I release the safety catch and hold my breath. He waits another minute or so with his arms akimbo, looking like he doesn't give a shit. His heart is deep under the skin and flesh, perfectly aligned between my sights.

"You're never going to shoot, you fucking coward. Maybe if you shoot the cross-eyed sergeant, he won't go shoving it up your ass anymore, eh?"

I lower the gun, and he makes another one of his contemptuous gestures. "*Yallah,* I'm going, Cocksucker. I'll bass by here tomorrow. When do they let you guard these barrels again? Ten till two? See you then." He starts walking off towards one of the back alleys, but suddenly he stops and smirks: "Give Abutbul regards from the *Hamas,* eh? Tell him we really abologize for that brick."

The rifle is back up in a flash, and I zero in till I have him right between my sights again. His shirt is buttoned up by now, but his heart is still mine. Then somebody knocks me down. I keel over in the sand, and suddenly I see Eli, the sergeant in charge. "Are you out of your mind, Meyer?" he screams. "What the hell do you think you're doing, standing there like some damn cowboy with your weapon smeared over your cheek? What do you think this is? The fucking Wild West or something, so you can go around putting slugs through anyone who comes along?"

"Dammit, Eli, I wasn't going to shoot him. I just wanted to scare him," I say, avoiding his gaze.

"You want to scare him?" he yells again, shaking me by the straps of my flak vest. "Then tell him ghost stories. What's the big idea—aiming at him with your gun cocked, and the safety off, no less?"

"Looks like Cross-Eyed isn't going to bush it up your ass today, Homo," I hear the Arab shout. "Good for you, Cross-Eyed, punch him one for me too."

"You've got to learn to ignore them," Eli says, out of breath as he gets off me. "Got that, Meyer?" He switches to a menacing whisper. "You've got to learn to relax. Because if I ever see you pulling anything like this again, I'm going to see to it personally that they bring you up on charges."

That night, somebody phoned from the hospital to say that the operation hadn't gone so well, and that Jacky would probably remain a vegetable.

"Just so long as we learn to ignore them," I spit out at Eli. "If this goes on, we'll wind up ignoring them for good, like Jacky."

"What's your beef, Meyer?" Suddenly Eli stands up straight. "You think I don't care about Abutbul? He was as much my friend as yours, you know. You think I don't feel like taking the jeep right this minute and going from house to house and dragging them out and putting bullets through their fucking heads, every last one of them? But if I did that, I'd be just like them. Don't you get it? You don't understand anything, do you?" But suddenly I really do understand. Much better than he does.

He's standing there, in the middle of the alleyway, about twenty meters away from me, his *kaffiyeh* over his face.

"Good morning, Cocksucker," he yells at me. "Great morning," I whisper back.

"How's Abutbul doing, Homo?" he yells at me. "Did you give him regards from the *Hamas?*" I let my vest fall to the ground. Then I take off my helmet.

"What's up, Homo?" he shouts. "Your brain all screwed up from so much fucking with Cross-Eyed?" I tear the wrapping off my field dressing, and tie it across my face. The only thing still showing is my eyes. I take the rifle, cock it, and make sure the safety's on. I grab the butt with both hands, swing the rifle over my head a few times, and suddenly let go. It flies through the air, barely scraping the ground, then lands about midway between us. Now I'm just like him. Now I've got a chance of winning too.

"That's for you, *ya majnun,*" I scream at him. For a second he just stares at me, puzzled. Then he makes a dash for the weapon. He lurches right at it, and I race towards him. He's faster than me. He'll get to it before me. But I'll win, because now I'm just like him, and with the rifle in his hand, he'll be just like me. His mother and his sisters will make it with Jews, his friends will vegetate in hospital beds, and he'll stand there facing me like a fucking asshole with a rifle in his hand, and won't be able to do a thing. How can I possibly lose?

He picks up the rifle, with me less than five meters away, and releases the safety lock. One knee on the ground, he aims and pulls the trigger. And then he discovers what I've discovered in this hell-hole over the past month: the rifle is worth shit. Three and half kilos of scrap metal. Totally useless. No point in even trying. I reach him before he so much as makes it up off the ground, and kick him hard, right in the muzzle. As he buckles over, I drag him up by the hair and pull off his *kaffiyeh.* I look him in the eye. Then I grab that face and bang it against a telephone pole like a raving maniac. Again and again and again. Let's see some cross-eyed sergeant push it up his ass now.

(1994)

—Translated by Miriam Shlesinger

About the Authors

~

Shmuel Yosef Agnon was the recipient of the 1966 Nobel Prize for Literature. He was born in Galicia in 1888. He immigrated to Jaffa in 1908, but spent the years 1913 through 1924 in Germany. In 1924 he returned to Jerusalem, where he lived until his death in 1970. Agnon was a prolific novelist and short-story writer from an early age. Called "a man of unquestionable genius" and "one of the great storytellers of our time," S. Y. Agnon is among the most effusively praised and widely translated Hebrew authors. His unique style and language have influenced the writing of subsequent generations of Hebrew writers.

Ehud Ben-Ezer was born in 1936 in Petah Tikva, where his family has been rooted since 1878. A kibbutz member for some time, he later studied philosophy and Kabbala (from Gershom Scholem) at the Hebrew University in Jerusalem. Ben-Ezer writes prose for children as well as fiction and nonfiction for adults, and is also a literary critic in the Hebrew press. A collection of his interviews with prominent Israeli writers, politicians, and intellectuals, *Unease in Zion,* was published by Quadrangle, New York, and *Hosni the Dreamer,* a picture book based on an old Arab tale, by Farrar, Strauss & Giroux. Often praised for his courageous writing, Ehud Ben-Ezer frequently broaches controversial social and erotic issues. His prose style is naturalistic and strongly atmospheric, plunging the reader into the scents and sounds of the individual worlds Ben-Ezer creates. Whether cynical or optimistic, writing fiction or nonfiction for children or for adults, Ben-Ezer's work presents a credible and authentic portrait of the Israeli experience.

Yosef Haim Brenner was born in the Ukraine in 1881. He received a religious education, but joined the Jewish socialist movement as a young man and later became a Zionist. After serving in the Russian army for three years, he left in 1904 for London, where he worked as a typesetter and for two years edited *HaMe'orer,* a Hebrew publication. Immigrating in 1909 to Eretz-Israel, he worked for a short period as an agricultural laborer, later settling in Jerusalem and then Jaffa, where he wrote, edited, and taught. Essayist, critic, and commentator, translator and novelist, Brenner was the most prominent literary figure in Eretz-Israel in his day, and in effect shifted the center of Hebrew literary activities away from Europe. He was killed by Arab rioters in 1921. His work continues to have a strong influence on the development of Hebrew writing.

Jacob Buchan was born in Austria in 1946 and came to Israel with his parents at the age of two. He is a graduate of the Tel Aviv Art School. In addition to contributing short stories to magazines and newspapers, he has worked as a graphic artist. He lives with his family in a village in central Israel. In his first novel, *Jacob's Life,* Jacob Buchan describes the world of the generation that fought in the 1973 Yom Kippur War. The war he describes is an almost surrealistic scene of alienation, in which the soul of the hero gradually disintegrates. In the story, Buchan returns to the image of the perennial hero of classic Hebrew literature—that of a seeker and a wanderer—but his language is unusually direct. Buchan's style is naturalistic and realistic, although his narratives rely heavily on allegory.

Etgar Keret was born in Tel Aviv in 1967. He had a column in the Jerusalem weekly *Kol Ha'ir* and a comic strip in a local Tel Aviv paper. He began publishing short stories in the press in 1991, and his first collection, *Pipelines,* appeared in 1992. He subsequently published a collection of short stories entitled *Missing Kissinger,* which met with critical acclaim, and two comic books for which he wrote the text. Keret writes comedy for Israeli television, and lectures at Tel Aviv University's School of Film. Keret's innovative style has had a profound influence on Israel's upcoming generation of writers.

Sami Michael was born in Baghdad in 1926. In 1948 he was declared a leftist activist and was forced to escape to Iran. From there he made his way to Israel. He studied Arabic literature and psychology at Haifa University and began writing prose, in both Hebrew and Arabic. For twenty-five years a hydrologist for the Ministry of Agriculture, he is both a novelist and playwright. Sami

Michael's novels, for both children and adults, cover the wide range of interlinked relationships between Jews and Arabs, Moslems and Christians, nationalists and communists, and men and women, both in Baghdad and Israel, as well as the story of Michael's own coming of age as a political radical in Baghdad. He is considered one of the few Hebrew writers who understands the mentality of the various parties in the Middle East.

Amos Oz was born in 1939 in Jerusalem. At the age of fifteen he went to live on a kibbutz. He studied philosophy and literature at the Hebrew University in Jerusalem, and was visiting fellow at Oxford University, author-in-residence at the Hebrew University, and writer-in-residence at The Colorado College. An author of prose for both children and adults, as well as an essayist, he has been widely translated and is internationally acclaimed. He lives in the southern town of Arad and teaches literature at Ben Gurion University of the Negev. Amos Oz has rooted his writing in the tempestuous history of his homeland. Several common threads run through his writing, both fiction and nonfiction: examining human nature, recognizing its frailty but glorying in its variety, Oz consistently makes the plea for an end to ambivalence, for dialogue, for channeling of passions toward faith in the future. With an economy of words, Oz presents the people of Israel, its political tribulations, and biblical landscape.

Esther Raab was born in Petakh-Tikva in 1894. Her father, Yehuda Raab (Ben-Ezer), was one of the founders of that first Jewish settlement in Palestine in 1878. The poet Harold Schimmel, who translated a selection of her poems, writes in his introduction: "Like her father who plows the first furrow in the Land of Israel [then Palestine], Esther is the first native-born Hebrew woman-poet." Her first book of verse, *Kimshonim* [Thistles], appeared in 1930. She wrote poems and short stories until her death in 1981. Her poetry describes the unique landscapes of her childhood and a woman's desire to love and to be loved. Her life alternated between "Days of Gall and Honey," her own words in one of her poems and the title of a recent biography written by her nephew, Ehud Ben-Ezer.

Shin Shifra was born in Israel in 1931. She studied Kabbalah, literature, and education at the Hebrew University in Jerusalem and at Tel Aviv University. She is a well-known poet and has taught creative writing for years. Shifra has published poetry, prose, translations of

Sumarian and Akkadian literature, interviews with prominent Israeli writers, and literary criticism. Among her volumes of poetry are *A Woman's Song, The Next Step,* and *Poems of the Desert,* and she has also published a collection of short stories entitled *Sand Street.* In cooperation with Professor Jacob Klein, she recently published an acclaimed anthology of Mesopotamian literature in Hebrew translation titled *In Those Distant Days.*

Moshe Smilansky was born in 1874 in the Ukraine. He came to Eretz-Israel in 1890, farmed in Hadera, Rishon le-Zion, and finally Rehovot, and was one of the organizers of the Jewish Battalion in the First World War. He was a founder and for many years president of the Eretz-Israel Farmers' Association and editor of its weekly. He died in 1953. His stories are about the life of the Arabs in the country, the life of the Jewish settlers, and memories of life in the Jewish communities in the Ukraine. His tales of Arab life (written under the pseudonym "Hawaja Moussa") are marked by their romantic approach to an exotic environment; they tell of ardent love, bravery, Bedouin raids, and the patriarchal system. In his stories of the life of the early Jewish settlers, he tells of the reawakening of the national spirit, the heroism, and the difficulties of adjustment to the rigors of settling in a new country, and of the devoted love of the settlers' wives. He also published memoirs and articles on the problems of settlement, Jewish labor, defense, and the Arab question.

Benjamin Tammuz was born in Russia in 1919. He immigrated to Tel Aviv at the age of five. He studied at Tel Aviv University and later attended the Sorbonne, where he studied art history. After working as the literary editor of the Hebrew daily *Ha'Aretz* for nine years, he spent four years in London as Israel's cultural attaché. A prolific author of both children's and adult literature, his writing is marked by a variety of styles, moving from lyricism to satire, and he is noted for his ability to evoke the inner workings of the individual. The tension between Judaism and the Israeli entity, as well as the inherent tension between art and reality, figure prominently in his writing. Benjamin Tammuz died in 1989.

A. B. Yehoshua was born in 1936 in Jerusalem and today lives in Haifa. He studied Hebrew literature and philosophy at the Hebrew University in Jerusalem. He has taught at high school and university levels, and lectured in Paris while living there from 1963 to 1967. He is a professor of literature at Haifa University. Best known as a novelist and playwright, A. B. Yehoshua is among the most widely recognized Israeli authors internationally. His writing has established him as one of Israel's foremost authors, a novelist with an outstanding gift for capturing the mood of contemporary Israel. In a style that has been called "anti–stream of consciousness," he explores the animal instincts that threaten the facade of civilized people and examines their isolation from each other, their community, and themselves.

S. Yizhar was born in 1916 in the agricultural town of Rehovot to a family of Russian immigrants, members of the Zionist pioneer intelligentsia. His father, Ze'ev Smilansky, was a farmer and publicist, as was his father's uncle, the writer Moshe Smilansky. Yizhar fought in the 1948 War of Independence and held a Knesset (Israeli Parliament) seat for seventeen years as a member of the political parties headed by David Ben-Gurion. He has taught literature and education, and was appointed professor at Tel Aviv University. Yizhar's first story appeared in 1938. It was followed by several volumes of fiction, among them the novella *Shayara Shel Hatsot* [The Midnight Convoy] and *Y'mai Ziklag* [The Days of Ziklag], a long novel about the Israeli War of Independence published in 1958, whose difficult style and outspoken iconoclasm became a literary cause célèbre. The story "The Prisoner" was written shortly after the War of Independence. It takes place in the late summer of 1948, a period when the Jewish forces were on the offensive throughout most of the country.

Bibliography

BEN-EZER, EHUD. *Unease in Zion.* New York and Jerusalem: Quadrangle/ Jerusalem Academic Press, 1974.

———. "The Arab Question in Israeli Literature." A talk with Ehud Ben-Ezer. *Shdemot* 6, 1976.

———. "War and Siege in Israeli Literature (1948–1967)." *The Jerusalem Quarterly*, no. 2, winter 1977.

———. "War and Siege in Hebrew Literature After 1967." *The Jerusalem Quarterly*, no. 9, fall 1978.

———. "Landscapes and Borders: A Sense of Siege in Israeli Literature." *Borders*, The Israeli Museum (Jerusalem), cat. no. 199, spring-summer, 1980; see also, *Shofar: An Interdisciplinary Journal of Jewish Studies* 7, no. 3, spring 1989.

———. "The Eye of the Beholder." *Spectrum*, December 1984.

———. "Arab Images in Hebrew Literature, 1900–1930." *New Outlook*, Special Supplement, appendix III, Tel Aviv, 1985, March 1986.

———. "Brenner and the Arab Question." *Modern Hebrew Literature*, spring-summer, 1987.

———. *Bemoledet Haga'aguim Hamenugadim* [At the Homeland of the Contradictory Longings], "The Arab in Israeli Fiction, a Hebrew Anthology," selected and introduced by Ehud Ben-Ezer. Series editor, Shin Shifra. Tel Aviv: The Hebrew Writers Association & Zmora-Bitan Publishers, 1992.

GOVRIN, NURIT. "Enemies or Cousins? . . . Somewhere in Between. The Arab Problem and Its Reflections on Hebrew Literature: Developments, Trends and Examples." *Shofar: An Interdisciplinary Journal of Jewish Studies* 7, no. 3, spring 1989.

DOMB, RISA. *The Arab in Hebrew Prose, 1911–1948.* London: Vallentine, Mitchell, 1982.

PATTERSON, DAVID. *A Darkling Plain: Jews and Arabs in Modern Hebrew Literature.* The Yarnton Trust for the Oxford Centre for Postgraduate Hebrew Studies, St. Giles, Oxford.

RAMRAS-RAUCH, GILA. "Moshe Smilansky: Utopia and Reality." *Shofar: An Interdisciplinary Journal of Jewish Studies* 7, no. 3, spring 1989.

———. *The Arab in Israeli Literature.* Bloomington and London: Tauris/Indiana University Press, 1989.

SHAKED, GERSHON. "The Arab in Israeli Fiction." *Modern Hebrew Literature,* fall 1989.

SOMEKH, SASSON, ET AL. "The Image of the Arab in Hebrew and Translated Literature as Taught in the Israeli High School." *New Outlook,* Special Supplement, Tel Aviv, 1985, March 1986.

About the Book

〜

Arabs, the Arab question, and the exotic romanticism of living in the Middle East first appeared in the emerging Hebrew literature in the late nineteenth century. In *Sleepwalkers and Other Stories*, noted Israeli writer and literary critic Ehud Ben-Ezer presents short stories and excerpts from novels, dating from 1906 to 1994, that trace the place of Arabs in Jewish Israeli consciousness.

The thirteen stories richly show how Jewish writers have presented dramatically differing interpretations of Arabs, ranging from visions of courageous Bedouins astride their noble horses, to fellow Semites, to a moral problem, to an existential nightmare. The tension created between the Arab perceived as an external threat and the Arab minority at home characterizes the rhythm of both modern Israeli history and modern Hebrew literature.

Ehud Ben-Ezer, twice a winner of Israel's Prime Minister Prize for Literature, writes fiction and nonfiction for adults, as well as children's stories (most recently *Hosni the Dreamer: An Arabian Tale*). His numerous publications include *The Quarry* (film version released in 1990). He is also a well-known literary critic in the Hebrew press.